THE AUSTRALIAN
Women's Weekly

BEST OF
Slow
COOKING

THE AUSTRALIAN WOMEN'S WEEKLY
TRIPLE TESTED
TEST KITCHEN

Contents

TAKE IT SLOW & STEADY 4

BEEF 6

LAMB 40

PORK 66

VEGETABLES 90

GLOSSARY 114

INDEX 117

Take it
SLOW & STEADY

There's something wonderful about the aroma of a slow-cooked meal. Slow cookers are perfect for this way of cooking.

Most slow cookers recommend you brown the meat first. Browning the meat enhances the flavour and gives your meat a beautiful rich colour. Do this in a heated, oiled, large frying pan, adding the meat in batches and turning it so that it browns evenly. Be sure to have the pan on a high heat; too low and it will stew. If you are pushed for time, meat/vegetables can be browned the night before. Once everything is browned, put it in a sealable container, along with any juices, and refrigerate until the next day.

Before using a slow cooker, read the manufacturer's instructions for use, and never leave a slow cooker on and unattended for safety reasons.

SLOW COOKING WORKS BEST WITH THE LESS EXPENSIVE CUTS OF MEAT. LONG, SLOW COOKING WILL TENDERISE EVEN THE TOUGHEST CUTS.

The best cuts of meat to use are

BEEF Topside, oyster, blade, round, chuck, skirt, gravy beef.

VEAL Osso buco, shanks, shoulder.

LAMB Neck chops, boneless shoulder, shanks, boneless forequarter.

PORK Forequarter chops, neck, belly, shoulder.

CHICKEN Any pieces on the bone, such as maryland, drumsticks, thigh.

Other types of meat, such as venison, kangaroo, goat, rabbit, hare, etc, are suitable to use in the slow cooker. Seafood is generally not recommended as it toughens quickly, however there are many recipes for sauces that can be cooked in the slow cooker, with the seafood added just before serving.

BEEF

BOURBON-GLAZED BEEF RIBS

PREP + COOK TIME 8 HOURS 30 MINUTES **SERVES** 4

1 medium brown onion (150g), chopped finely

5 cloves garlic, chopped coarsely

½ cup (140g) tomato sauce (ketchup)

½ cup (140g) sweet chilli sauce

⅓ cup (80ml) light soy sauce

½ cup (125ml) bourbon

½ cup (175g) honey

8 beef short ribs (2kg)

1 Combine onion, garlic, sauces, bourbon and honey in a 4.5-litre (18-cup) slow cooker. Add beef; turn to coat in mixture. Cook, covered, on low, about 8 hours. Carefully remove beef from cooker; cover to keep warm.

2 Transfer sauce to a large frying pan; bring to the boil. Boil, skimming fat from surface, for 10 minutes or until sauce reduces to 2 cups.

3 Spoon sauce over beef to serve.

SUITABLE TO FREEZE At the end of step 1.
SERVING SUGGESTION Thinly sliced fried potatoes.

BEEF CASSEROLE WITH CHEESY HERB DUMPLINGS

PREP + COOK TIME 8 HOURS 30 MINUTES **SERVES** 6

1kg (2 pounds) gravy beef

1 tablespoon olive oil

1 large brown onion (200g), chopped coarsely

2 cloves garlic, crushed

2 tablespoons tomato paste

400g (12½ ounces) canned whole peeled tomatoes

1 cup (250ml) beef stock

½ cup (125ml) dry red wine

4 sprigs fresh thyme

250g (8 ounces) button mushrooms, halved

1 cup (150g) self-raising flour

50g (1½ ounces) cold butter, chopped finely

2 tablespoons finely chopped fresh flat-leaf parsley

⅔ cup (80g) coarsely grated vintage cheddar

½ cup (125ml) buttermilk, approximately

1 Cut beef into 3cm (1¼-inch) pieces. Heat oil in a large frying pan over medium-high heat. Cook beef, in batches, until browned. Transfer to a 4.5-litre (18-cup) slow cooker.

2 Add onion and garlic to same pan; cook, stirring, for 5 minutes or until onion softens. Add paste, tomatoes, stock, wine and thyme to pan; bring to the boil. Transfer mixture to slow cooker; add mushrooms.

3 Cook, covered, on low, about 7 hours. Remove and discard thyme sprigs. Season to taste.

4 Meanwhile, place flour in a medium bowl; rub in butter. Add half the parsley and half the cheddar; stir to combine. Stir in enough buttermilk to make a soft, sticky dough. Drop rounded tablespoons of the dumpling mixture, 2cm (¾ inch) apart, on top of casserole in cooker; scatter with remaining cheddar. Cook, covered, for 1 hour or until dumplings are cooked through. Scatter with remaining parsley to serve.

SUITABLE TO FREEZE At the end of step 3.
SERVING SUGGESTION Steamed green beans or spinach.
TIP We used a cabernet-style wine in this recipe.

BEEF, DATE AND SPINACH TAGINE

PREP + COOK TIME 8 HOURS 35 MINUTES **SERVES** 6

1.2kg (2½ pounds) beef blade steak, chopped coarsely

¼ cup (35g) plain (all-purpose) flour

1 tablespoon olive oil

1 large red onion (300g), chopped finely

2 cloves garlic, crushed

1 teaspoon ground cinnamon

1 teaspoon ground cumin

½ teaspoon ground ginger

½ teaspoon ground turmeric

¼ teaspoon saffron threads

1 cup (250ml) beef stock

400g (12½ ounces) canned diced tomatoes

¾ cup (100g) seeded dried dates

315g (10 ounces) spinach, trimmed, shredded coarsely

1 tablespoon thinly sliced preserved lemon rind

⅓ cup (45g) coarsely chopped roasted unsalted pistachios

1 Toss beef in flour to coat, shake off excess. Heat half the oil in a large frying pan; cook beef, in batches, until browned. Transfer to a 4.5-litre (18-cup) slow cooker.

2 Heat remaining oil in same pan; cook onion and garlic, stirring, until onion softens. Add spices; cook, stirring, until fragrant. Add ½ cup of the stock; cook, stirring, until mixture boils.

3 Transfer onion mixture to cooker with remaining stock and tomatoes; stir to combine. Cook, covered, on low, about 8 hours.

4 Add dates, spinach and half the preserved lemon rind; cook, covered, on high, for 10 minutes or until spinach wilts. Season to taste.

5 Sprinkle tagine with nuts and remaining preserved lemon rind.

SUITABLE TO FREEZE At the end of step 3.
SERVING SUGGESTION Steamed couscous or rice.
TIPS Beef shin or chuck steak could also be used. Preserved lemon is available at delis and some supermarkets. Remove and discard the flesh, wash the rind, then use it as the recipe directs.

OSSO BUCO WITH MIXED MUSHROOMS

PREP + COOK TIME 8 HOURS 50 MINUTES **SERVES** 6

6 large pieces beef osso buco (1.7kg)

¼ cup (35g) plain (all-purpose) flour

2 tablespoons olive oil

1 large brown onion (200g), chopped coarsely

1 cup (250ml) marsala

1½ cups (375ml) beef stock

¼ cup (60ml) worcestershire sauce

2 tablespoons wholegrain mustard

2 sprigs fresh rosemary

185g (6 ounces) swiss brown mushrooms, sliced thickly

155g (5 ounces) portabello mushrooms, cut into 8 wedges

155g (5 ounces) oyster mushrooms, chopped coarsely

½ cup (125ml) pouring cream

¼ cup (35g) gravy powder

2 tablespoons water

½ cup coarsely chopped fresh flat-leaf parsley

1   Coat beef in flour, shake off excess. Heat half the oil in a large frying pan; cook beef, in batches, until browned all over. Remove from pan.
2   Heat remaining oil in same pan; cook onion, stirring, until onion softens. Add marsala; bring to the boil. Add onion mixture to a 4.5-litre (18-cup) slow cooker; stir in stock, sauce, mustard and rosemary. Place beef in cooker, fitting pieces upright and tightly packed in a single layer. Add mushrooms to cooker. Cook, covered, on low, about 8 hours.
3   Carefully remove beef from cooker; cover to keep warm. Add cream and combined gravy powder and the water to cooker; cook, covered, on high, for 10 minutes or until mixture thickens slightly. Stir in parsley; season to taste.
4   Serve beef with mushroom sauce.

NOT SUITABLE TO FREEZE.
SERVING SUGGESTION Kumara, potato or celeriac mash and a green leafy salad.
TIPS Ask the butcher for either veal or beef shin (osso buco) – veal will be smaller than beef, in which case you will need about 12 pieces to serve six people. You can use a mixture of mushrooms as we have, or just one variety with a good robust flavour – you will need a total of 500g (1 pound).

PULLED BEEF WITH BARBECUE SAUCE

PREP + COOK TIME 8 HOURS 45 MINUTES
SERVES 6

Pulled beef, or pork, comes from pulling extremely tender pieces of meat apart – rather than cutting it into slices – usually with two forks, which separates the meat into strands. Low, slow cooking is required to get meat tender enough to pull apart into pieces.

2 cloves garlic, crushed

1 fresh long red chilli, chopped finely

2 tablespoons dark brown sugar

1½ cups (420g) tomato sauce (ketchup)

1½ tablespoons worcestershire sauce

2 tablespoons cider vinegar

750g (1½-pound) piece beef rump

6 long crusty bread rolls

1 Place garlic, chilli, sugar, sauces and vinegar in a 4.5-litre (18-cup) slow cooker. Stir well to combine; add beef and turn to coat in mixture. Cook, covered, on low, about 8 hours.
2 Carefully remove beef from cooker; shred meat coarsely using two forks.
3 Transfer sauce mixture to a large saucepan, bring to the boil over medium heat. Boil, uncovered, for 10 minutes or until thickened. Stir in beef.
4 Split rolls in half lengthways, fill with beef and sauce mixture.

SUITABLE TO FREEZE At the end of step 3.
SERVING SUGGESTION Fill rolls with beef mixture, lettuce, finely grated cheddar and pickled peppers.

MASSAMAN BEEF CURRY

PREP + COOK TIME 8 HOURS 45 MINUTES
SERVES 6

2 tablespoons peanut oil

2 large brown onions (400g), cut into thin wedges

1kg (2 pounds) gravy beef, chopped coarsely

⅔ cup (200g) massaman curry paste

1 cup (250ml) coconut milk

1 cup (250ml) chicken stock

2 cinnamon sticks

2 dried bay leaves

3 medium potatoes (600g), chopped coarsely

½ cup (70g) roasted unsalted peanuts

2 tablespoons brown sugar

1 tablespoon fish sauce

⅓ cup lightly packed fresh coriander (cilantro) leaves

1 lime, cut into wedges

1 Heat half the oil in a large frying pan; cook onion, stirring, for 10 minutes or until browned lightly. Transfer to a 4.5-litre (18-cup) slow cooker.
2 Heat remaining oil in same pan; cook beef, in batches, until browned. Add paste; cook, stirring, for 1 minute or until fragrant. Transfer to cooker.
3 Add coconut milk, stock, cinnamon, bay leaves, potato and nuts to cooker. Cook, covered, on low, about 8 hours.
4 Discard cinnamon sticks. Stir in sugar and sauce. Serve curry sprinkled with coriander; accompany with lime wedges.

NOT SUITABLE TO FREEZE.
TIP Chuck steak is also suitable for this recipe.

CHINESE BRAISED BEEF CHEEKS

PREP + COOK TIME 8 HOURS 30 MINUTES **SERVES** 8

1 large orange

4 green onions (scallions), trimmed, cut into 6cm (2½-inch) lengths

6 cloves garlic, crushed

10cm (4-inch) piece fresh ginger (50g), sliced thickly

1½ cups (375ml) chinese cooking wine

1 cup (250ml) soy sauce

1 cup (220g) firmly packed brown sugar

½ teaspoon sesame oil

5 star anise

2 cinnamon sticks

8 beef cheeks (2.5kg)

1 fresh long red chilli, sliced thinly

2 green onions (scallions), extra, trimmed, sliced thinly lengthways

½ cup firmly packed fresh coriander (cilantro) leaves

1 Using a vegetable peeler, peel three wide strips of rind from orange.
2 Combine rind, onion, garlic, ginger, wine, sauce, sugar, oil, star anise and cinnamon in a 4.5-litre (18-cup) slow cooker. Stir until the sugar dissolves. Add beef; turn to coat in mixture. Cook, covered, on low, about 8 hours.
3 Serve beef with a little cooking liquid; sprinkle with chilli, extra onion and coriander.

SUITABLE TO FREEZE At the end of step 2.
SERVING SUGGESTION Steamed rice.
TIP You may need to order beef cheeks in advance from the butcher.

MEXICAN BEEF CHILLI MOLE

PREP + COOK TIME 8 HOURS 45 MINUTES SERVES 4

1kg (2 pounds) beef chuck steak, cut into 3cm (1¼-inch) cubes

2 cups (500ml) beef stock

2 cups (500ml) water

3 chipotle peppers in adobo sauce, chopped finely

4 rindless bacon slices (260g), chopped coarsely

1 medium brown onion (150g), chopped finely

4 cloves garlic, crushed

2 tablespoons tomato paste

439g (14 ounces) canned black beans, rinsed, drained

410g (13 ounces) canned tomato puree

2 teaspoons each ground cumin, ground coriander and sweet smoked paprika

¼ teaspoon chilli powder

½ teaspoon ground cinnamon

2 tablespoons finely grated mexican chocolate

⅔ cup (80g) grated manchego cheese

1 fresh jalapeño chilli, sliced thinly

2 green onions (scallions), sliced thinly

1 Combine beef, stock, the water, chipotle, bacon, brown onion, garlic, paste, beans, puree and spices in a 4.5-litre (18-cup) slow cooker. Cook, covered, on low, about 8 hours.

2 Stir chocolate into cooker; season to taste.

3 Serve beef topped with cheese, jalapeño and green onion.

SUITABLE TO FREEZE At the end of step 2.

TIPS Chipotle in adobo sauce and mexican chocolate are available from specialist delicatessens and grocers. If chipotle in adobo sauce is unavailable use 2-3 tablespoons hot Mexican-style chilli sauce (adding enough to suit your taste). If mexican chocolate is unavailable use dark (semi-sweet) chocolate. Manchego is an aged, hard, intensely flavoured Spanish cheese. It is available from Spanish delicatessens and specialist cheese shops; substitute haloumi or fetta if not available. If fresh jalapeño chillies are unavailable, use slices of bottled pickled jalapeño.

OXTAIL STEW WITH RED WINE AND PORT

PREP + COOK TIME 9 HOURS 15 MINUTES **SERVES** 8

2kg (4 pounds) oxtails, cut into 5cm (2-inch) pieces

2 tablespoons plain (all-purpose) flour

2 tablespoons vegetable oil

12 brown pickling onions (480g)

2 medium carrots (240g), chopped coarsely

1 stalk celery (150g), trimmed, sliced thickly

8 cloves garlic, peeled

1½ cups (375ml) dry red wine

2 cups (500ml) port

2 cups (500ml) beef stock

4 sprigs fresh thyme

1 dried bay leaf

½ cup lightly packed fresh flat-leaf parsley leaves

1 Trim excess fat from oxtail; toss oxtail in flour to coat, shake off excess. Heat half the oil in a large frying; cook oxtail, in batches, until browned. Transfer to a 4.5-litre (18-cup) slow cooker.
2 Meanwhile, peel onions, leaving root ends intact.
3 Heat remaining oil in same pan; cook onions, carrot, celery and garlic, stirring, for 5 minutes or until vegetables are browned lightly. Transfer to cooker. Add wine and port to pan; bring to the boil. Boil, uncovered, until reduced to 1 cup. Transfer to cooker with stock, thyme and bay leaf. Cook, covered, on low, about 8 hours.
4 Discard thyme and bay leaf. Remove oxtail; cover to keep warm. Cook sauce, uncovered, on high, for 30 minutes or until thickened. Skim fat from surface.

SUITABLE TO FREEZE At the end of step 4. Pack oxtail into freezer-proof container; pour sauce over, leaving 2.5cm (1-inch) space to allow for expansion. Seal, label and freeze for up to 3 months.
SERVING SUGGESTION Potato, celeriac or parsnip puree.

BEEF RIB BOURGUIGNON

PREP + COOK TIME 8 HOURS 30 MINUTES
SERVES 4

12 shallots (300g)

200g (6½ ounces) button mushrooms

200g (6½ ounces) swiss brown mushrooms

4 rindless bacon slices (260g), cut into 5cm (2-inch) lengths

3 cloves garlic, sliced thinly

2 fresh thyme sprigs

2 fresh bay leaves

1½ cups (375ml) dry red wine

3 cups (750ml) beef stock

2 tablespoons tomato paste

1.2kg (2½ pounds) beef short ribs

½ cup finely chopped fresh flat-leaf parsley

1 Place shallots, mushrooms, bacon, garlic, thyme, bay leaves, wine, stock, paste and beef in a 4.5-litre (18-cup) slow cooker. Cook, covered, on low, about 8 hours.
2 Discard thyme and bay leaves. Stir in half the parsley; season to taste. Serve topped with remaining parsley and accompany with crusty bread, if you like.

NOT SUITABLE TO FREEZE.
SERVING SUGGESTION Mashed potato or steamed baby new potatoes.
TIP Cut the shallots in half if they are large.

BEER AND THYME BEEF CHEEKS

PREP + COOK TIME 10 HOURS 30 MINUTES
SERVES 6

16 baby onions (400g)

3 stalks celery (450g), trimmed, chopped coarsely

400g (12½ ounces) baby carrots, trimmed

4 sprigs fresh thyme

1½ cups (375ml) beer

1 cup (250ml) beef stock

¼ cup (70g) tomato paste

2 tablespoons worcestershire sauce

1 tablespoon brown sugar

1 tablespoon wholegrain mustard

2kg (4 pounds) trimmed beef cheeks

150g (4½ ounces) green beans, trimmed

1 Peel onions, leaving root ends intact. Combine onions with celery, carrots, thyme, beer, stock, paste, sauce, sugar and mustard in a 5-litre (20-cup) slow cooker. Add beef; turn to coat in mixture. Cook, covered, on low, about 9½ hours.
2 Discard thyme. Add beans to cooker; cook, covered, on low, for 30 minutes. Season to taste.
3 Serve beef sprinkled with extra fresh thyme, if you like.

SUITABLE TO FREEZE At the end of step 2.
SERVING SUGGESTION Creamy mashed potato or cheesy polenta.
TIP You will need 1 bunch of baby carrots. They may also be sold as 'dutch' carrots.

BEEF POT ROAST

PREP + COOK TIME 8 HOURS 30 MINUTES **SERVES** 4

¼ cup (60ml) olive oil

4 small potatoes (180g), unpeeled, halved

375g (12-ounce) piece unpeeled pumpkin, cut into 4 wedges

8 baby onions (200g), halved

375g (12 ounces) baby carrots

250g (8 ounces) jerusalem artichokes (sunchokes)

750g (1½-pound) piece beef blade steak

1 tablespoon wholegrain mustard

2 teaspoons smoked paprika

2 teaspoons finely chopped fresh rosemary

1 garlic clove, crushed

1½ cups (375ml) beef stock

½ cup (125ml) dry red wine

2 tablespoons balsamic vinegar

¼ cup (35g) gravy powder

2 tablespoons water

1 Heat 2 tablespoons of the oil in a large frying pan; cook potato, pumpkin and onion, in batches, until browned all over. Place vegetables in a 4.5-litre (18-cup) slow cooker with carrots and artichokes.

2 Heat 2 teaspoons of the remaining oil in same pan; cook beef until browned all over. Remove beef from pan; spread with combined mustard, paprika, rosemary, garlic and remaining oil.

3 Place beef on vegetables in slow cooker; pour over combined stock, wine and vinegar. Cook, covered, on low, about 8 hours.

4 Remove beef and vegetables from cooker; cover beef, stand 10 minutes before slicing thinly. Cover vegetables to keep warm.

5 Meanwhile, blend gravy powder with the water in a small bowl until smooth. Stir gravy mixture into liquid in slow cooker; cook, covered, on high, for 10 minutes or until gravy is thickened slightly. Season to taste. Strain gravy.

6 Serve beef with gravy and vegetables.

NOT SUITABLE TO FREEZE.
SERVING SUGGESTION Steamed green beans or broccoli.
TIPS We used nicola potatoes and jap pumpkin in this recipe. Jerusalem artichokes can be hard to find; add swede, parsnip or turnip to the pot roast instead. Gravy powder is an instant gravy mix made with browned flour. Plain flour can be used for thickening instead.

COCONUT CURRIED BEEF

PREP + COOK TIME 10 HOURS 45 MINUTES **SERVES** 4

1kg (2 pounds) diced beef

2 tablespoons thai yellow curry paste

1⅔ cups (410ml) coconut milk

2 cups (500ml) beef stock

1 tablespoon finely grated fresh ginger

3 cloves garlic, crushed

2 medium brown onions (300g), cut into thin wedges

2 fresh kaffir lime leaves

8 fresh curry leaves

2 tablespoons fish sauce

2 tablespoons grated palm sugar

150g (4½ ounces) snow peas

2 tablespoons finely chopped peanuts, roasted

¼ cup firmly packed fresh thai basil leaves

1 fresh long red chilli, sliced thinly

1 Place beef, paste and coconut milk in a 4.5-litre (18-cup) slow cooker; stir until paste dissolves.

2 Add stock, ginger, garlic, onion, lime leaves, curry leaves, sauce and sugar to cooker. Cook, covered, on high, about 2 hours. Reduce to low; cook a further 8 hours. Season to taste.

3 Discard lime leaves. Stir in snow peas; cook, covered, on low, for 10 minutes or until peas are tender. Season to taste. Serve beef topped with nuts, basil and chilli.

NOT SUITABLE TO FREEZE.
SERVING SUGGESTION Steamed jasmine rice or fresh rice noodles accompanied with lime wedges.

CHILLI CON CARNE

PREP + COOK TIME 8 HOURS 45 MINUTES SERVES 6

1 tablespoon olive oil

1 large brown onion (200g), chopped finely

2 cloves garlic, crushed

750g (1½ pounds) minced (ground) beef

1 teaspoon ground cumin

1½ teaspoons dried chilli flakes

1 cup (250ml) beef stock

⅓ cup (95g) tomato paste

820g (28 ounces) canned crushed tomatoes

1 tablespoon finely chopped fresh oregano

800g (1½ pounds) canned kidney beans, rinsed, drained

½ cup loosely packed fresh coriander (cilantro) leaves

6 flour tortillas, warmed

1 Heat oil in a large frying pan; cook onion and garlic, stirring, until onion softens. Add beef, cumin and chilli; cook, stirring, until browned. Transfer to a 4.5-litre (18-cup) slow cooker. Stir in stock, paste, tomatoes and oregano. Cook, covered, on low, about 8 hours.

2 Add beans; cook, covered, on high, for 30 minutes or until hot. Season to taste.

3 Sprinkle chilli con carne with coriander; serve with tortillas.

SUITABLE TO FREEZE At the end of step 1.
SERVING SUGGESTION Steamed rice and a dollop of sour cream, plus a green leafy salad.

SUITABLE TO FREEZE At the end of step 3.
SERVING SUGGESTION Steamed rice.

VIETNAMESE BEEF BRISKET

PREP + COOK TIME 9 HOURS 45 MINUTES **SERVES** 4

1.5kg (3 pounds) beef brisket, trimmed, cut into 5cm (2-inch) pieces

1 large brown onion (200g), sliced thinly

3 cloves garlic, crushed

1 tablespoon finely grated fresh ginger

1 fresh long red chilli, sliced thinly

2 x 10cm (4-inch) sticks fresh lemon grass (40g), halved lengthways

2 fresh kaffir lime leaves, bruised

2 star anise

1 cinnamon stick

2 tablespoons grated palm sugar

¼ cup (60ml) fish sauce

¼ cup (60ml) dark soy sauce

3 cups (750ml) beef stock

1 large red capsicum (bell pepper) (350g), chopped coarsely

125g (4 ounces) baby corn, halved

150g (4½ ounces) snake beans, chopped coarsely

⅓ cup (45g) coarsely chopped roasted unsalted peanuts

⅓ cup loosely packed fresh coriander (cilantro) leaves

1 Combine beef, onion, garlic, ginger, chilli, lemon grass, lime leaves, star anise, cinnamon, sugar, sauces, stock, capsicum and corn in a 5-litre (20-cup) slow cooker. Cook, covered, on low, about 9 hours.
2 Add beans to cooker; cook, covered, 30 minutes.
3 Discard lemon grass, lime leaves, star anise and cinnamon; season to taste.
4 Sprinkle beef with nuts and coriander.

BEEF AND VEGETABLE SOUP

PREP + COOK TIME 9 HOURS 45 MINUTES **SERVES** 4

1kg (2 pounds) gravy beef, trimmed, cut into
2.5cm (1-inch) pieces

1 garlic clove, crushed

1 medium brown onion (150g), cut into
1cm (½-inch) pieces

2 stalks celery (300g), trimmed, cut into
1cm (½-inch) pieces

2 medium carrots (240g), cut into 1cm (½-inch) pieces

2 medium potatoes (400g), cut into 1cm (½-inch) pieces

400g (12½ ounces) canned diced tomatoes

1 litre (4 cups) water

2 cups (500ml) beef stock

2 dried bay leaves

1 cup (120g) frozen peas

⅓ cup coarsely chopped fresh flat-leaf parsley

1   Combine beef, garlic, onion, celery, carrot,
potato, tomatoes, the water, stock and bay leaves
in a 5-litre (20-cup) slow cooker. Cook, covered,
on low, about 9 hours.
2   Add peas to cooker; cook, covered, a further
30 minutes.
3   Discard bay leaves. Season to taste.
4   Serve soup sprinkled with parsley.

SUITABLE TO FREEZE At the end of step 3.
SERVING SUGGESTION Thick slices of crusty bread.

CORIANDER BEEF CURRY

PREP + COOK TIME 8 HOURS 30 MINUTES **SERVES** 6

6 fresh long green chillies

7.5cm (3-inch) piece fresh ginger (35g), chopped coarsely

4 cloves garlic, chopped coarsely

2 medium tomatoes (300g), chopped coarsely

1 tablespoon tomato paste

2 teaspoons sea salt flakes

2½ cups firmly packed fresh coriander (cilantro) leaves

1½ tablespoons vegetable oil

1.5kg (3 pounds) chuck steak or gravy beef, cut into 5cm (2-inch) pieces

400ml canned coconut cream

1 Coarsely chop four of the chillies. Thinly slice remaining chillies, reserve.
2 Blend or process chopped chilli, ginger, garlic, tomato, paste, salt and 2 cups of the coriander until smooth. Reserve ½ cup of the coriander paste; cover, then refrigerate.
3 Heat 1 tablespoon of the oil in a large frying pan over medium-high heat; cook beef, in batches, until browned. Transfer beef to a 4.5-litre (18-cup) slow cooker.
4 Add remaining coriander paste and 1 cup of the coconut cream to cooker; stir to combine. (Refrigerate remaining coconut cream.) Cook, covered, on low, about 8 hours. Season to taste.
5 Heat remaining oil in a small frying pan; cook sliced chilli, stirring, for 2 minutes or until softened. Drizzle curry with remaining coconut cream; top with the reserved coriander paste, chilli and remaining coriander.

SUITABLE TO FREEZE At the end of step 4.
SERVING SUGGESTION Steamed jasmine rice.
TIP You will need about 2 large bunches of coriander.

OLD-FASHIONED CURRIED SAUSAGES

PREP + COOK TIME 8 HOURS 20 MINUTES **SERVES** 6

12 thick beef sausages (1.8kg)

1 tablespoon vegetable oil

2 medium brown onions (300g), sliced thinly

2 tablespoons mild curry powder

400g (12½ ounces) canned diced tomatoes

1 cup (250ml) beef stock

1 cup (250ml) water

4 medium potatoes (800g), unpeeled, cut into thick wedges

1 cup (120g) frozen peas, thawed

½ cup (80g) sultanas

1 Place sausages in a large saucepan, add enough cold water to cover sausages; bring to the boil. Boil, uncovered, about 2 minutes; drain.
2 Heat oil in same pan; cook onion, stirring, until softened. Add curry powder; cook, stirring, until fragrant. Remove from heat; stir in tomatoes, stock and the water.
3 Place potatoes in a 4.5-litre (18-cup) slow cooker; top with sausages and onion mixture. Cook, covered, on low, about 8 hours.
4 Stir in peas and sultanas. Season to taste.

NOT SUITABLE TO FREEZE.
SERVING SUGGESTION Crusty bread.

BORSCHT

PREP + COOK TIME 8 HOURS 50 MINUTES SERVES 6

60g (2 ounces) butter

2 medium brown onions (300g), chopped finely

500g (1 pound) beef chuck steak, cut into large chunks

1 cup (250ml) water

750g (1½ pounds) beetroot (beets), peeled, chopped finely

2 medium potatoes (400g), chopped finely

2 medium carrots (240g), chopped finely

4 small tomatoes (360g), chopped finely

1 litre (4 cups) beef stock

⅓ cup (80ml) red wine vinegar

3 dried bay leaves

4 cups (320g) finely shredded cabbage

2 tablespoons coarsely chopped fresh flat-leaf parsley

½ cup (120g) sour cream

1 Melt half the butter in a large frying pan; cook onion, stirring, until soft. Place onion in a 4.5-litre (18-cup) slow cooker. Melt remaining butter in same pan; cook beef, stirring, until browned all over. Place beef in cooker. Add the water to the same pan; bring to the boil, then add to slow cooker with beetroot, potato, carrot, tomato, stock, vinegar and bay leaves. Cook, covered, on low, about 8 hours.

2 Discard bay leaves. Remove beef from soup; shred using two forks. Return beef to soup with cabbage; cook, covered, on high, for 20 minutes or until cabbage is wilted. Stir in parsley.

3 Serve soup topped with sour cream.

SUITABLE TO FREEZE At the end of step 1.

LAMB

FETTA, LEMON AND HERB ROLLED LAMB

PREP + COOK TIME 8 HOURS 45 MINUTES **SERVES** 6

180g (5½ ounces) persian fetta in oil

¼ cup coarsely chopped fresh oregano

¼ cup coarsely chopped fresh mint

¼ cup coarsely chopped fresh basil

2 teaspoons finely grated lemon rind

2 tablespoons balsamic vinegar

1.5kg (3-pound) boneless lamb leg

1   Drain fetta reserving 2 tablespoons of the oil.
2   Combine fetta, herbs, rind and half the vinegar in a medium bowl. Season to taste.
3   Open out lamb and place on a board, fat-side down. Slice through the thickest part of the lamb horizontally, without cutting all the way through. Open out the flap to form one large even piece; spread fetta mixture over lamb. Roll lamb up to enclose the stuffing, securing with kitchen string at 2cm (¾-inch) intervals.
4   Heat half the reserved oil in a large frying pan over medium-high heat; cook lamb, turning, until browned. Transfer to a 4.5-litre (18-cup) slow cooker.
5   Combine remaining reserved oil and vinegar in a small bowl; brush over lamb. Cook, covered, on low, about 8 hours.

NOT SUITABLE TO FREEZE.
SERVING SUGGESTION Roasted wedges of pumpkin and fresh garden peas sprinkled with extra herbs.
TIPS Persian fetta is a soft, creamy cheese marinated in a blend of olive oil, garlic, herbs and spices. Ask the butcher to butterfly the lamb for you.

LAMB BIRYANI-STYLE

PREP + COOK TIME 9 HOURS (+ STANDING) SERVES 8

40g (1½ ounces) ghee

½ cup (40g) flaked almonds

2 large brown onions (400g), sliced thinly

1 tablespoon vegetable oil

1.2kg (2½ pounds) boneless lamb shoulder, chopped coarsely

20g (¾ ounce) ghee, extra

4 cloves garlic, crushed

5cm (2-inch) piece fresh ginger (25g), grated

2 fresh long green chillies, sliced thinly

2 teaspoons each ground cumin and ground coriander

3 teaspoons garam masala

¾ cup (200g) Greek-style yoghurt

½ cup coarsely chopped fresh coriander (cilantro)

¼ cup coarsely chopped fresh mint

1 litre (4 cups) water

pinch saffron threads

2 tablespoons hot milk

2 cups (400g) basmati rice

1 lime, cut into wedges

½ cup loosely packed fresh coriander (cilantro) leaves, extra

1 Heat half the ghee in a large frying pan; cook nuts, stirring, until browned lightly. Remove from pan. Heat remaining ghee in same pan; cook onion, stirring, for 10 minutes or until soft and browned lightly. Remove from pan.
2 Heat oil in same pan; cook lamb, in batches, until browned. Transfer to a 4.5-litre (18-cup) slow cooker. Heat extra ghee in same pan; cook garlic, ginger, chilli and spices, stirring, until fragrant. Remove from heat; stir in yoghurt, chopped herbs and half the onion mixture. Transfer to cooker with half the water. Cook, covered, on low, about 8 hours. Season to taste.
3 Meanwhile, sprinkle saffron over hot milk in a small bowl; stand 15 minutes.
4 Wash rice under cold water until water runs clear; drain. Combine rice and the remaining water in a medium saucepan, cover; bring to the boil. Reduce heat; simmer, covered, for 8 minutes or until rice is tender. Season to taste.
5 Spoon rice over lamb in cooker; drizzle with milk mixture. Top with nuts and remaining onion mixture; cook, covered, for 30 minutes or until heated through.
6 Serve with lime wedges; sprinkle with extra coriander leaves.

NOT SUITABLE TO FREEZE.
SERVING SUGGESTION Raita (minted yoghurt and cucumber).
TIP Biryani is a rice dish made with spices and meat, chicken, fish or vegetables. There are many versions as this delicious recipe is a favourite across the Middle-East and India.

LAMB SHANK, FENNEL AND VEGETABLE SOUP

PREP + COOK TIME 10 HOURS 30 MINUTES **SERVES** 6

1 tablespoon olive oil

4 french-trimmed lamb shanks (1kg)

1 medium brown onion (150g), chopped coarsely

2 baby fennel bulbs (260g), sliced thinly

2 medium carrots (240g), chopped coarsely

4 cloves garlic, crushed

2 fresh small red thai (serrano) chillies, chopped finely

2 teaspoons each ground cumin and ground coriander

1 teaspoon each ground cinnamon and caraway seeds

pinch saffron threads

1.5 litres (6 cups) water

2 cups (500ml) beef stock

400g (12½ ounces) canned diced tomatoes

400g (12½ ounces) canned chickpeas (garbanzo beans), drained, rinsed

¾ cup (90g) frozen baby peas

1 cup loosely packed fresh coriander (cilantro) leaves

1 Heat half the oil in a large frying pan; cook lamb, until browned all over, then place in a 4.5-litre (18-cup) slow cooker.
2 Heat remaining oil in same pan; cook onion, fennel, carrot, garlic and chilli, stirring, until onion softens. Add spices; cook, stirring, until fragrant. Place vegetable mixture into cooker. Stir in the water, stock, tomatoes and chickpeas. Cook, covered, on low, about 10 hours.
3 Remove lamb from cooker. When cool enough to handle, remove meat from bones, shred meat; discard bones. Stir meat and peas into cooker. Season to taste.
4 Serve soup sprinkled with coriander leaves.

SUITABLE TO FREEZE At the end of step 3.
SERVING SUGGESTION Lemon wedges, Greek-style yoghurt and crusty bread.

LAMB, KUMARA AND ALMOND CURRY

PREP + COOK TIME 8 HOURS 45 MINUTES
SERVES 4

1.2kg (2½-pound) boneless lamb leg, cut into
5cm (2-inch) pieces

800g (1½ pounds) kumara (orange sweet potato),
cut into 5cm (2-inch) pieces

1 large brown onion (200g), sliced thinly

3 cloves garlic, crushed

1 fresh long red chilli, chopped finely

2 teaspoons each garam masala and ground cumin

400g (12½ ounces) canned diced tomatoes

400ml canned coconut milk; reserve 2 tablespoons

250g (8 ounces) spinach, trimmed, shredded coarsely

½ cup (60g) ground almonds

⅓ cup (45g) toasted slivered almonds

⅓ cup loosely packed fresh coriander (cilantro) leaves

1 Combine lamb, kumara, onion, garlic, chilli, spices, tomatoes and coconut milk in a 5-litre (20-cup) slow cooker. Cook, covered, on low, about 8 hours.
2 Add spinach and ground almonds to cooker; cook, uncovered, on high, for 5 minutes or until spinach wilts. Season to taste.
3 Drizzle curry with reserved coconut milk and sprinkle with slivered almonds and coriander.

SUITABLE TO FREEZE At the end of step 1.
SERVING SUGGESTION Steamed basmati rice.

LAMB AND ROSEMARY STEW

PREP + COOK TIME 8 HOURS 45 MINUTES
SERVES 4

1.2kg (2½ pounds) lamb neck chops

⅓ cup (50g) plain (all-purpose) flour

2 tablespoons olive oil

1 cup (250ml) dry red wine

3 small brown onions (240g), sliced thickly

3 medium potatoes (600g), sliced thickly

2 medium carrots (240g), sliced thickly

2 tablespoons tomato paste

2 tablespoons finely chopped rosemary

1 cup (250ml) beef stock

1 Toss lamb in flour to coat; shake off excess. Heat half the oil in a large frying pan over medium-high heat; cook lamb, in batches, until browned. Transfer to a 4.5-litre (18-cup) slow cooker.
2 Add wine to same pan; bring to the boil. Boil, stirring occasionally, for 5 minutes or until liquid is reduced by half. Transfer to cooker. Add onion, potato, carrot, paste, rosemary and stock. Cook, covered, on low, about 8 hours. Season to taste.
3 Divide lamb and vegetables among plates. Spoon over a little cooking liquid to serve.

SUITABLE TO FREEZE At the end of step 2.
SERVING SUGGESTION Peas or green beans.
TIP We used a shiraz-style wine in this recipe.

LAMB AND EGGPLANT CURRY WITH CASHEWS

PREP + COOK TIME 8 HOURS 45 MINUTES **SERVES** 6

¼ cup (60ml) vegetable oil

6 baby eggplants (360g), cut into 3cm (1¼-inch) thick slices

6 french-trimmed lamb shanks (1.5kg)

1 large brown onion (200g), chopped finely

3 cloves garlic, grated

5cm (2-inch) piece fresh ginger (25g), grated

3 fresh long red chillies, sliced thinly

2 teaspoons each ground cumin, ground coriander and garam masala

400g (12½ ounces) canned diced tomatoes

2 cups (500ml) beef stock

1 tablespoon sesame seeds

¼ cup (50g) toasted salted cashews

1 tablespoon desiccated coconut

¾ cup (200g) Greek-style yoghurt

¼ cup lightly packed fresh coriander (cilantro) leaves

1 Heat 1 tablespoon of the oil in a large frying pan over medium heat; cook eggplant, in batches, until browned. Transfer to a 4.5-litre (18-cup) slow cooker.

2 Heat 1 tablespoon of the oil in the same pan over medium heat; cook lamb, in batches, until browned. Transfer to cooker.

3 Heat remaining oil in same pan over medium heat; cook onion, stirring, for 5 minutes or until softened. Add garlic, ginger, chilli and spices; cook, stirring, for 1 minute or until fragrant. Stir in tomatoes and stock; bring to the boil. Transfer to cooker. Cook, covered, on low, about 8 hours.

4 Meanwhile, dry-fry seeds, nuts and coconut together until fragrant but not coloured; cool. Blend or process until finely ground. Stir nut mixture into curry. Season to taste.

5 Serve curry topped with yoghurt and coriander.

SUITABLE TO FREEZE At the end of step 3.
SERVING SUGGESTION Steamed basmati rice and asian greens.
TIP Sprinkle curry with fried chillies before serving, if you like. Thinly slice 2 fresh long red chillies, heat 2 teaspoons oil in a small frying pan, cook chilli, stirring, until softened.

GREEK-STYLE DILL AND LEMON LAMB SHOULDER

PREP + COOK TIME 8 HOURS 45 MINUTES **SERVES** 6

1 tablespoon olive oil

2kg (4-pound) lamb shoulder, bone in

1 medium lemon (140g)

4 cloves garlic, crushed

2 teaspoons dried greek oregano

1 tablespoon coarsely chopped fresh dill

800g (1½ pounds) potatoes, cut into thick wedges

1 cup (280g) bottled passata

2 cups (500ml) salt-reduced chicken stock

50g (1½ ounces) seeded black olives

2 tablespoons fresh dill sprigs, extra

1 Heat oil in a large frying pan over medium heat; cook lamb until browned all over. Remove from pan.

2 Meanwhile, finely grate rind from lemon; reserve lemon. Combine garlic, rind, oregano and chopped dill in a small bowl. Rub mixture over lamb.

3 Place potato over the base of a 4.5-litre (18-cup) slow cooker. Pour passata and stock over potatoes. Top with lamb. Cook, covered, on low, about 8 hours.

4 Carefully remove lamb and potato from cooker; shred lamb coarsely using two forks. Cover to keep warm.

5 Pour cooking liquid into a medium saucepan; bring to the boil. Boil, uncovered, for 10 minutes or until liquid is reduced by half. Add olives; cook until heated through. Season to taste.

6 Cut reserved lemon into wedges. Serve lamb with potato, pan juices and lemon wedges; sprinkle with extra dill.

NOT SUITABLE TO FREEZE.
SERVING SUGGESTION Steamed broad beans.
TIPS Ask the butcher to separate the shank from the shoulder, leaving it attached; this will help it fit into the cooker. We used dutch cream potatoes in this recipe, as they hold their shape well. Passata is strained tomato puree available from supermarkets.

CASSOULET

PREP + COOK TIME 8 HOURS 45 MINUTES **SERVES** 6

2 tablespoons olive oil

3 thick pork sausages (360g)

100g (3-ounce) piece speck, rind removed, cut into 3cm (1¼-inch) pieces

900g (1¾ pounds) boneless lamb shoulder, cut into 3cm (1¼-inch) pieces

1 large brown onion (200g), chopped finely

1 dried bay leaf

5 cloves garlic, chopped finely

800g (1½ pounds) canned diced tomatoes

1 cup (250ml) water

2 tablespoons tomato paste

4 x 400g (12½ ounces) canned white beans, rinsed, drained

2 tablespoons finely chopped fresh flat-leaf parsley

1 Heat half the oil in a large frying pan over medium-high heat; cook sausages and speck, turning, until browned. Transfer to a 4.5-litre (18-cup) slow cooker.

2 Heat same pan over medium-high heat; cook lamb, in batches, until browned. Transfer to cooker. Drain fat from pan.

3 Heat remaining oil in same pan over medium heat; cook onion and bay leaf, stirring, for 5 minutes or until onion softens. Add garlic; cook, stirring, for 1 minute or until fragrant. Transfer to cooker.

4 Add tomatoes, the water, paste and beans to cooker. Cook, covered, on low, about 8 hours. Season to taste.

5 Serve cassoulet sprinkled with parsley.

SUITABLE TO FREEZE At the end of step 4.
SERVING SUGGESTION Lightly toast some breadcrumbs and combine with chopped parsley; sprinkle over cassoulet to serve.
TIP There are many regional variations of cassoulet in France. For special occasions, add two confit duck marylands. Pan fry them until hot and browned, place on top of hot cassoulet before sprinkling with parsley.

LAMB BIRRIA (SPICY MEXICAN LAMB STEW)

PREP + COOK TIME 10 HOURS 45 MINUTES **SERVES** 4

3 teaspoons mexican chilli powder

1 teaspoon each dried oregano and ground cumin

¼ teaspoon each ground cloves and ground cinnamon

1 tablespoon finely grated fresh ginger

3 cloves garlic, sliced thinly

700g (1½ pounds) trimmed lamb rump steaks, cut into 3cm (1¼-inch) cubes

2 sprigs fresh thyme

2 fresh bay leaves

2 cups (500ml) salt-reduced chicken stock

1 cup (250ml) water

1 medium brown onion (150g), chopped coarsely

285g (9-ounce) jar whole roasted piquillo peppers, drained, chopped

410g (13 ounces) canned crushed tomatoes

½ cup (85g) seeded prunes, halved

½ cup loosely packed fresh coriander (cilantro) leaves

1 Place chilli, oregano, cumin, cloves, cinnamon, ginger and garlic in a 4.5-litre (18-cup) slow cooker. Add lamb; toss to coat in mixture.
2 Add thyme, bay leaves, stock, the water, onion, peppers and tomatoes. Cook, covered, on low, about 10 hours. Season to taste.
3 Remove and discard thyme and bay leaves. Stir in prunes. Cook, covered, on low, for 10 minutes or until prunes soften. Serve topped with coriander.

SUITABLE TO FREEZE At the end of step 2.
SERVING SUGGESTION Grilled corn tortillas and lime wedges.

MOROCCAN LAMB WITH HONEY

PREP + COOK TIME 8 HOURS 45 MINUTES
SERVES 4

400g (12½ ounces) baby carrots, trimmed

600g (1¼ pounds) baby new potatoes

8 spring onions (200g), trimmed

1 cup (250ml) chicken stock

1.5kg (3-pound) lamb shoulder

2 tablespoons honey

2 tablespoons vegetable oil

3 cloves garlic, crushed

2 teaspoons fennel seeds

1 teaspoon each ground cinnamon, ginger and cumin

¼ teaspoon cayenne pepper

1 Combine carrots, potatoes, onions and stock in a 5-litre (20-cup) slow cooker.
2 Score lamb at 2.5cm (1-inch) intervals. Combine honey, oil, garlic, seeds and spices in a small bowl. Rub honey mixture over lamb. Place lamb on top of vegetables in cooker. Cook, covered, on low, about 8 hours.
3 Coarsely shred or slice lamb; serve with vegetables and some of the cooking liquid.

NOT SUITABLE TO FREEZE.
SERVING SUGGESTION Steamed green beans, peas, spinach or silver beet.

TOMATO AND BALSAMIC LAMB STEW

PREP + COOK TIME 8 HOURS 45 MINUTES
SERVES 4

8 lamb neck chops (1.4kg)

400g (12½ ounces) canned diced tomatoes

1 medium red onion (170g), sliced thinly

2 cloves garlic, crushed

1 cup (250ml) beef stock

½ cup (125ml) dry red wine

⅓ cup (80ml) balsamic vinegar

½ cup (75g) coarsely chopped sun-dried tomatoes

¼ cup loosely packed fresh basil leaves

2 sprigs fresh thyme

340g (11-ounce) jar marinated artichoke hearts, drained

2 teaspoons cornflour (cornstarch)

1 tablespoon water

¼ cup loosely packed fresh baby basil leaves, extra

1 Combine lamb, tomatoes, onion, garlic, stock, wine, vinegar, sun-dried tomatoes and herbs in a 5-litre (20-cup) slow cooker. Cook, covered, on low, about 8 hours.

2 Discard thyme from cooker; stir in artichokes. Combine cornflour with the water in a small cup; stir into cooker. Cook, covered, on high, for 10 minutes or until thickened slightly. Season to taste.

3 Serve stew sprinkled with extra basil.

SUITABLE TO FREEZE At the end of step 1.
SERVING SUGGESTION Mashed potato or creamy polenta.
TIP We used red wine but you can use white wine if preferred.

SICILIAN MEATBALLS IN SPICY TOMATO SAUCE

PREP + COOK TIME 8 HOURS 45 MINUTES **SERVES** 4

700g (1½ pounds) bottled passata

410g (13 ounces) canned crushed tomatoes

1 medium brown onion (150g), chopped finely

45g (1½ ounces) canned anchovies, drained

¼ teaspoon dried chilli flakes

3 cloves garlic, sliced thinly

1 cup (250ml) chicken stock

2 cups (500ml) water

⅓ cup fresh oregano leaves, torn

600g (1¼ pounds) minced (ground) lamb

1 cup (70g) stale breadcrumbs

2 tablespoons pine nuts, chopped

1 tablespoon finely grated lemon rind

¼ cup (40g) sultanas, chopped

¼ cup (20g) finely grated parmesan

⅓ cup loosely packed small fresh basil leaves

1 Place passata, tomatoes, onion, anchovies, chilli, garlic, stock, the water and half the oregano in a 4.5-litre (18-cup) slow cooker. Stir to combine.
2 Using your hands, combine lamb, breadcrumbs, pine nuts, rind, sultanas, parmesan and remaining oregano in a large bowl; roll level tablespoons of mixture into balls. Transfer to cooker. Cook, covered, on low, about 8 hours. Season to taste.
3 Serve meatballs sprinkled with basil.

SUITABLE TO FREEZE At the end of step 2.
SERVING SUGGESTION Pasta, creamy polenta or mashed potato.
TIP Uncooked meatballs and sauce can be frozen separately, then cooked at a later stage.

LAMB SHANK AND SPINACH KORMA CURRY

PREP + COOK TIME 8 HOURS 30 MINUTES **SERVES** 6

6 french-trimmed lamb shanks
(1.5kg)

400g (12½ ounces) canned crushed
tomatoes

1 large brown onion (200g),
sliced thickly

300ml pouring cream

100g (3 ounces) baby spinach leaves

1 cup (120g) frozen peas

KORMA PASTE

1 tablespoon cumin seeds

3 cloves garlic, quartered

5cm (2-inch) piece fresh ginger
(25g), grated finely

⅓ cup (50g) toasted cashew nuts

¼ cup (60ml) tomato sauce
(ketchup)

¼ cup coarsely chopped coriander
(cilantro) root and stem mixture

2 tablespoons desiccated coconut

1 tablespoon garam masala

2 teaspoons each ground coriander,
ground turmeric and sea salt flakes

¼ cup (60ml) vegetable oil

1   Make korma paste.
2   Combine lamb, tomatoes, onion, cream and paste in a 4.5-litre
(18-cup) slow cooker. Cook, covered, on low, about 8 hours.
3   Add spinach and peas to cooker; cook, covered, for 10 minutes or
until heated through.

KORMA PASTE Place cumin in a small frying pan; cook, stirring, for 1 minute
or until fragrant. Remove from heat. Blend or process cumin with remaining
ingredients until smooth.

SUITABLE TO FREEZE At the end of step 2. Korma paste can be frozen separately.
SERVING SUGGESTION Steamed basmati rice, yoghurt and naan bread.

LANCASHIRE HOT POT

PREP + COOK TIME 8 HOURS 30 MINUTES **SERVES** 4

800g (1½ pounds) boneless lamb shoulder, cut into 3cm (1¼-inch) pieces

⅓ cup (50g) plain (all-purpose) flour

2 tablespoons olive oil

2 medium brown onions (300g), chopped coarsely

2 cloves garlic, chopped coarsely

½ cup (125ml) dry red wine

2 medium carrots (240g), chopped coarsely

200g (6½ ounces) button mushrooms, halved

1 tablespoon fresh thyme leaves

1 tablespoon worcestershire sauce

500g (1 pound) potatoes

1 Toss lamb in flour to coat, shake off excess. Heat half the oil in a large frying pan over medium-high heat; cook lamb, in batches, until browned. Transfer to a 4.5-litre (18-cup) slow cooker.
2 Heat remaining oil in same pan; cook onion and garlic, stirring, for 5 minutes or until onion softens. Transfer to cooker.
3 Heat same pan; add wine, bring to the boil. Transfer to cooker with carrot, mushrooms, thyme and sauce; stir to combine.
4 Thinly slice potatoes. Arrange potato slices, slightly overlapping, over lamb mixture. Cook, covered, on low, about 8 hours. Season to taste.

NOT SUITABLE TO FREEZE.
SERVING SUGGESTION Buttered peas.
TIPS We used a merlot-style wine in this recipe. If you have a mandoline, use it to cut the potatoes into paper-thin slices, otherwise, use a very sharp knife.

PORK

HAM AND GREEN LENTIL SOUP WITH GREMOLATA

PREP + COOK TIME 8 HOURS 30 MINUTES **SERVES** 6

1.8kg (3½-pounds) meaty ham hocks

½ cup (100g) French-style green lentils

1 tablespoon vegetable oil

2 medium brown onions (300g), chopped finely

2 medium carrots (240g), chopped finely

2 stalks celery (300g), trimmed, chopped finely

1 teaspoon fresh thyme leaves

2 cups (500ml) salt-reduced chicken stock

1.5 litres (6 cups) water

GREMOLATA

2 cloves garlic, crushed

¼ cup finely chopped fresh flat-leaf parsley

2 teaspoons finely grated lemon rind

1 Rinse ham hocks. Place in a 4.5-litre (18-cup) slow cooker.

2 Rinse lentils; drain well.

3 Heat oil in a medium frying pan over medium heat; cook onion, stirring, for 5 minutes or until softened. Transfer onion to cooker with carrot, celery, thyme, lentils, stock and the water. Cook, covered, on low, about 8 hours.

4 Carefully remove ham hocks from cooker. When cool enough to handle, remove and discard skin and bones. Shred meat finely using two forks. Return meat to cooker. Season to taste.

5 When almost ready to serve, make gremolata; sprinkle over soup.

GREMOLATA Combine ingredients in a small bowl.

SUITABLE TO FREEZE At the end of step 4.
SERVING SUGGESTION Crusty bread.
TIP Make sure the ham hocks are not too large to fit in the slow cooker. Ask the butcher to cut them, if necessary.

SWEET AND SOUR ITALIAN PORK WITH CAPSICUM

PREP + COOK TIME 8 HOURS 45 MINUTES **SERVES** 6

1.5kg (3-pound) piece pork scotch fillet (neck)

2 tablespoons olive oil

2 medium red capsicums (bell peppers) (400g)

2 medium brown onions (300g), chopped finely

1 stalk celery (150g), trimmed, chopped coarsely

2 cloves garlic, chopped finely

¼ cup (55g) caster (superfine) sugar

½ cup (125ml) red wine vinegar

2 tablespoons tomato paste

½ cup (125ml) chicken stock

¼ cup (40g) sultanas

2 tablespoons pine nuts

2 tablespoons chopped fresh flat-leaf parsley

1   Tie pork with kitchen string at 2cm (¾-inch) intervals. Heat half the oil in a large frying pan over medium-high heat; cook pork until browned. Transfer to a 4.5-litre (18-cup) slow cooker.

2   Meanwhile, cut capsicums lengthways into eighths; discard seeds and membranes.

3   Heat remaining oil in same pan over medium heat; cook onion, celery and garlic, stirring occasionally, for 5 minutes or until softened. Add sugar; cook, stirring occasionally, for 10 minutes or until golden and caramelised. Add vinegar; bring to the boil. Stir in paste and stock; bring to the boil, then pour over pork. Add sultanas and capsicum to cooker. Cook, covered, on low, about 8 hours.

4   Carefully remove pork from cooker; transfer to serving plate, cover to keep warm.

5   Meanwhile, toast pine nuts in a dry frying pan, stirring continuously over medium heat until just golden. Remove immediately from pan. Spoon sauce over pork. Serve sprinkled with pine nuts and parsley.

NOT SUITABLE TO FREEZE.
SERVING SUGGESTION Mashed potato or polenta.
TIP 'Agrodolce' is the Italian word used to describe the flavours in this dish. It means 'sour sweet'.

RIBOLLITA

PREP + COOK TIME 8 HOURS 45 MINUTES **SERVES** 6

1 ham hock (1kg)

1 medium brown onion (150g), chopped finely

2 stalks celery (300g), trimmed, sliced thinly

1 large carrot (180g), chopped finely

1 small fennel bulb (200g), sliced thinly

3 cloves garlic, crushed

400g (12½ ounces) canned diced tomatoes

2 sprigs fresh rosemary

½ teaspoon dried chilli flakes

2 litres (8 cups) water

375g (12 ounces) cavolo nero, shredded coarsely

400g (12½ ounces) canned cannellini beans, rinsed, drained

½ cup coarsely chopped fresh basil

250g (8 ounces) sourdough bread, crust removed

½ cup (40g) flaked parmesan

1   Combine ham hock, onion, celery, carrot, fennel, garlic, tomatoes, rosemary, chilli and the water in a 4.5-litre (18-cup) slow cooker. Cook, covered, on low, about 8 hours.

2   Remove ham hock from cooker; add cavolo nero and beans to soup. Cook, covered, on high, for 20 minutes or until cavolo nero is wilted.

3   Meanwhile, when ham hock is cool enough to handle, remove meat from bone; shred coarsely. Discard skin, fat and bone. Add meat and basil to soup; season to taste.

4   Break chunks of bread into serving bowls; top with soup and parmesan.

NOT SUITABLE TO FREEZE.

TIP   Ribollita [ree-boh-lee-tah] literally means 'reboiled'. This Tuscan soup was originally made by reheating leftover minestrone or vegetable soup and adding bread, white beans and vegetables such as carrot, zucchini, spinach and cavolo nero.

PEPPERED PORK CURRY

PREP + COOK TIME 8 HOURS 30 MINUTES
SERVES 4

1.2kg (2½ pounds) diced boneless pork shoulder

1 medium red onion (170g), sliced thinly

4 cloves garlic, crushed

1 tablespoon finely grated fresh ginger

2 tablespoons brown sugar

2 teaspoons cracked black pepper

1 cinnamon stick

2 teaspoons ground cumin

1 teaspoon ground fenugreek

½ teaspoon ground cardamom

1 cup (250ml) chicken stock

400g (12½ ounces) canned diced tomatoes

1 cup (280g) Greek-style yoghurt

150g (4½ ounces) baby spinach leaves

⅓ cup loosely packed fresh coriander (cilantro) leaves

1 Combine pork, onion, garlic, ginger, sugar, spices, stock, tomatoes and half the yoghurt in a 5-litre (20-cup) slow cooker. Cook, covered, on low, about 8 hours.
2 Discard cinnamon. Add spinach and remaining yoghurt to cooker; cook, uncovered, on high, for 5 minutes or until spinach wilts. Season to taste. Serve curry sprinkled with coriander; top with extra yoghurt, if you like.

SUITABLE TO FREEZE At the end of step 1.
SERVING SUGGESTION Steamed rice and warmed roti bread.

BOSTON BAKED BEANS

PREP + COOK TIME 10 HOURS 30 MINUTES
SERVES 4

1 large brown onion (200g), chopped finely

300g (9½-ounce) piece speck, rind removed, chopped finely

¼ cup (90g) golden syrup

⅓ cup (75g) firmly packed brown sugar

2 tablespoons dijon mustard

1 tablespoon worcestershire sauce

1 tablespoon hot chilli sauce

410g (13 ounces) canned crushed tomatoes

400g (12½ ounces) canned cannellini beans, rinsed, drained

400g (12½ ounces) canned butter beans, rinsed, drained

400g (12½ ounces) canned borlotti beans, rinsed, drained

3 cups (750ml) salt-reduced chicken stock

½ cup finely chopped fresh flat-leaf parsley

1 Place onion, speck, syrup, sugar, mustard, sauces, tomatoes, beans and stock in a 4.5-litre (18-cup) slow cooker. Cook, covered, on low, about 9 hours. Uncover, cook, on low, for 1 hour or until thickened slightly. Season to taste.
2 Serve beans sprinkled with parsley.

SUITABLE TO FREEZE At the end of step 1.
SERVING SUGGESTION Baby spinach leaves and crusty bread.
TIP Substitute golden syrup with treacle for a darker, richer mixture.

BEST-EVER BOLOGNESE SAUCE

PREP + COOK TIME 10 HOURS 40 MINUTES **SERVES** 6

1 tablespoon olive oil

125g (4-ounce) piece prosciutto, chopped finely

2 medium brown onions (300g), chopped finely

1 large carrot (180g), chopped finely

2 stalks celery (300g), trimmed, chopped finely

2 cloves garlic, crushed

500g (1 pound) minced (ground) pork

500g (1 pound) minced (ground) veal

1 cup (250ml) dry red wine

1½ cups (375ml) beef stock

¼ cup (70g) tomato paste

1kg (2 pounds) ripe tomatoes, peeled, seeded, chopped coarsely

⅓ cup finely chopped fresh basil

2 tablespoons finely chopped fresh oregano

1 Heat half the oil in a large frying pan; cook prosciutto, stirring, until crisp. Add onion, carrot, celery and garlic; cook, stirring, until vegetables soften. Transfer to a 4.5-litre (18-cup) slow cooker.
2 Heat remaining oil in same pan; cook pork and veal, stirring, until browned. Add wine; bring to the boil. Stir mince mixture into cooker with stock, paste and tomato; cook, covered, on low, about 10 hours.
3 Stir in herbs; cook, covered, on high, about 10 minutes. Season to taste.

SUITABLE TO FREEZE At the end of step 2.
SERVING SUGGESTION Spaghetti or your favourite pasta; top with shaved parmesan.
TIPS Prosciutto can be replaced with bacon. Fresh tomatoes can be replaced with 800g (1½ pounds) canned diced tomatoes.

SOY PORK WITH MUSHROOMS

PREP + COOK TIME 8 HOURS 30 MINUTES (+ STANDING) **SERVES** 4

1.2kg (2½-pound) boneless pork shoulder

2 cinnamon sticks

2 star anise

⅔ cup (160ml) soy sauce

½ cup (125ml) chinese cooking wine

¼ cup (55g) firmly packed brown sugar

1 fresh long red chilli, halved lengthways

5cm (2-inch) piece fresh ginger (25g), sliced thinly

6 cloves garlic, bruised

2½ cups (625ml) water

150g (4½ ounces) shiitake mushrooms, halved if large

150g (4½ ounces) oyster mushrooms, torn into large pieces

150g (4½ ounces) shimeji mushrooms

100g (3 ounces) enoki mushrooms

4 baby buk choy, halved or quartered

1 Place pork, cinnamon, star anise, sauce, cooking wine, sugar, chilli, ginger, garlic and the water in a 4.5-litre (18-cup) slow cooker. Cook, covered, on low, about 8 hours.
2 Carefully remove pork from cooker; stand, covered, 15 minutes. Using a slotted spoon, remove cinnamon, star anise, chilli, ginger and garlic from broth.
3 Add mushrooms and buk choy to cooker. Cook, covered, on high, for 15 minutes or until mushrooms are tender; season to taste. Serve slices of pork with vegetables and a little broth.

NOT SUITABLE TO FREEZE.
SERVING SUGGESTION Rice noodles.
TIP When adding the mushrooms and buk choy, don't worry if they aren't covered by the broth. They will shrink slightly whilst cooking. Place the buk choy on top of the mushrooms as this will ensure it stays green.

HONEY AND BALSAMIC BRAISED PORK

PREP + COOK TIME 8 HOURS **SERVES** 6

2 tablespoons olive oil

1.2kg (2½-pound) piece pork neck

9 shallots (225g), halved

1½ cups (375ml) chicken stock

⅓ cup (80ml) white balsamic vinegar

¼ cup (90g) honey

6 cloves garlic, peeled

2 sprigs fresh rosemary

1 cup (160g) seeded green olives

1   Heat oil in a large frying pan; cook pork until browned all over. Remove from pan.

2   Add shallots to same pan; cook, stirring, until browned all over. Add stock, vinegar and honey; bring to the boil.

3   Place garlic and rosemary in a 4.5-litre (18-cup) slow cooker; top with pork. Pour over shallot mixture; cook, covered, on low, about 7 hours.

4   Add olives; cook, covered, on low, about 30 minutes. Season to taste.

5   Remove pork; stand, covered, 10 minutes before slicing. Serve pork drizzled with sauce.

SUITABLE TO FREEZE At the end of step 3.
SERVING SUGGESTION Soft creamy polenta or mashed potato and wilted shredded cabbage.

MEXICAN PULL-APART PORK

PREP + COOK TIME 8 HOURS 30 MINUTES
SERVES 6

2 medium red capsicums (bell peppers) (400g), sliced thinly

2 medium brown onions (300g), sliced thinly

375g (12 ounces) bottled chunky mild tomato salsa

1 cup (280g) barbecue sauce

4 cloves garlic, crushed

3 teaspoons ground cumin

2 teaspoons cayenne pepper

1 teaspoon dried oregano

1kg (2-pound) boneless pork shoulder

12 large flour tortillas

1 cup (240g) sour cream

1 cup coarsely chopped fresh coriander (cilantro)

1 Combine capsicum, onion, salsa, sauce, garlic, spices and oregano in a 4.5-litre (18-cup) slow cooker; add pork, turn to coat in mixture. Cook, covered, on low, about 8 hours.
2 Carefully remove pork from cooker; shred meat using two forks. Return pork to cooker; stir gently. Season to taste.
3 Divide pork between tortillas. Serve topped with sour cream and coriander.

SUITABLE TO FREEZE At the end of step 2.
SERVING SUGGESTION Lime wedges.
TIP Peel the capsicum with a vegetable peeler if you don't like the skin peeling off when it's cooked.

ITALIAN PORK AND CAPSICUM RAGU

PREP + COOK TIME 8 HOURS 30 MINUTES
SERVES 8

2 tablespoons olive oil

1.6kg (3¼-pound) rindless boneless pork belly, chopped coarsely

4 Italian-style thin pork sausages (310g)

3 medium red capsicums (bell peppers) (600g), sliced thickly

2 medium brown onions (300g), sliced thinly

1.2kg (2½ pounds) canned white beans, drained, rinsed

6 cloves garlic, crushed

400g (12½ ounces) canned diced tomatoes

1¼ cups (310ml) salt-reduced chicken stock

1 tablespoon tomato paste

1 teaspoon dried oregano

½ teaspoon chilli flakes

¼ cup loosely packed fresh oregano leaves

1 Heat oil in a large frying pan; cook pork, in batches, until browned. Transfer to a 4.5-litre (18-cup) slow cooker.
2 Cook sausages in same pan until browned; transfer to cooker with capsicum, onion, beans, garlic, tomatoes, stock, paste, dried oregano and chilli. Cook, covered, on low, about 8 hours.
3 Skim fat from surface. Remove sausages from cooker; chop coarsely, return to cooker. Season to taste.
4 Serve ragù sprinkled with fresh oregano.

SUITABLE TO FREEZE At the end of step 3.
SERVING SUGGESTION Traditionally served with pasta.

RED PORK AND LYCHEE CURRY

PREP + COOK TIME 8 HOURS 30 MINUTES **SERVES** 4

565g (1¼ pounds) canned seeded lychees in syrup

1.5kg (3 pounds) pork belly ribs (spare ribs), rind removed, halved

1 large brown onion (200g), sliced thinly

2 cloves garlic, crushed

⅓ cup (100g) red curry paste

400ml canned coconut milk

½ cup (125ml) chicken stock

2 fresh kaffir lime leaves

2 tablespoons fish sauce

227g (7 ounces) canned water chestnut slices, rinsed, drained

125g (4 ounces) baby corn, halved

400g (12½ ounces) baby carrots, trimmed

200g (6½ ounces) snow peas, trimmed

⅓ cup (25g) fried shallots

⅓ cup loosely packed fresh coriander (cilantro) leaves

2 limes, cut into wedges

1 Drain lychees over a medium bowl; reserve ⅓ cup syrup. Refrigerate lychees.
2 Combine reserved syrup, pork, onion, garlic, paste, coconut milk, stock, lime leaves, sauce, water chestnut, corn and carrots in a 5-litre (20-cup) slow cooker. Cook, covered, on low, about 8 hours.
3 Discard lime leaves. Add lychees and snow peas to cooker; cook, uncovered, on high, for 5 minutes or until snow peas are tender. Season to taste. Serve curry sprinkled with shallots and coriander; accompany with lime wedges.

NOT SUITABLE TO FREEZE.
SERVING SUGGESTION Steamed jasmine rice.
TIP Fried shallots are available, canned or in cellophane bags, at Asian grocery stores; once opened, they will keep for months if tightly sealed. Make your own by thinly slicing shallots and shallow-frying in vegetable oil until crisp and golden-brown; drain on paper towel.

PORK VINDALOO

PREP + COOK TIME 8 HOURS 30 MINUTES SERVES 6

1.2kg (2½-pound) pork scotch fillet (neck)

2 large brown onions (400g), sliced thinly

5cm (2-inch) piece fresh ginger (25g), grated

2 cloves garlic, grated

400g (12½ ounces) canned diced tomatoes

½ cup (150g) vindaloo paste

2 tablespoons tomato paste

¾ cup (180ml) beef stock

½ cup loosely packed fresh coriander (cilantro) leaves

1 Cut pork into 3cm (1¼-inch) pieces; discard any excess fat.
2 Place pork, onion, ginger, garlic, tomatoes, pastes and stock in a 4.5-litre (18-cup) slow cooker. Cook, covered, on low, about 8 hours.
3 Sprinkle vindaloo with coriander.

SUITABLE TO FREEZE At the end of step 2.
SERVING SUGGESTION Steamed basmati rice and pappadums.
TIP The king of curries, the fiery Indian vindaloo, is from the former Portuguese colony of Goa. The name is derived from the Portuguese words for vinegar and garlic, the dish's primary ingredients, which give the dish its sweet/sour taste. Jars of vindaloo paste are available from supermarkets.

PORK AND CHILLI STEW

PREP + COOK TIME 8 HOURS 45 MINUTES **SERVES** 4

1 tablespoon olive oil

750g (1½ pounds) diced pork

1 medium red onion (170g), chopped finely

2 cloves garlic, chopped finely

1 medium red capsicum (bell pepper) (200g), chopped coarsely

500g (1 pound) baby new potatoes, quartered

35g (1-ounce) sachet chilli spice mix

400g (12½ ounces) canned corn kernels, rinsed, drained

800g (1½ pounds) canned diced tomatoes

2 limes

½ cup (140g) sour cream

2 fresh long green chillies, sliced thinly

¼ cup coarsely chopped fresh coriander (cilantro)

1   Heat oil in a large frying pan over medium-high heat; cook pork, turning, until browned. Transfer to a 4.5-litre (18-cup) slow cooker.
2   Place onion, garlic, capsicum, potato, spice mix, corn and tomatoes in cooker. Cook, covered, on low, about 8 hours.
3   Cut cheeks from limes. Divide pork mixture into serving bowls. Top with sour cream, chilli and coriander; accompany with lime cheeks.

SUITABLE TO FREEZE At the end of step 2.
SERVING SUGGESTION Tortilla chips.
TIPS If the potatoes are very small, halve them rather than cutting them into quarters. Most chilli spice mixes come as hot or mild; choose the heat level that you can tolerate.

VEGETABLES

SPLIT PEA AND CAPSICUM CURRY

PREP + COOK TIME 8 HOURS 30 MINUTES **SERVES** 4

1 medium brown onion (150g), sliced thinly

500g (1 pound) baby new potatoes, halved

1 large carrot (180g), halved, sliced thickly

1 medium red capsicum (bell pepper) (350g), chopped coarsely

1 medium yellow capsicum (bell pepper) (350g), chopped coarsely

⅓ cup (100g) mild indian curry paste

⅓ cup (85g) yellow split peas

⅓ cup (85g) green split peas

8 fresh curry leaves

2 tablespoons tomato paste

410g (13 ounces) canned crushed tomatoes

2 cups (500ml) vegetable stock

2 cups (500ml) water

150g (4½ ounces) sugar snap peas

500g (1 pound) spinach, trimmed, chopped coarsely

¾ cup (200g) Greek-style yoghurt

½ cup lightly packed fresh coriander (cilantro) leaves

1 Place onion, potato, carrot, capsicums, curry paste, split peas, curry leaves, tomato paste, tomatoes, stock and the water in a 4.5-litre (18-cup) slow cooker. Cook, covered, on low, about 8 hours. Season to taste.
2 Stir in sugar snap peas. Cook, uncovered, on low, for 10 minutes or until peas are tender. Stir in spinach. Serve curry topped with yoghurt and sprinkled with coriander.

NOT SUITABLE TO FREEZE.
SERVING SUGGESTION Steamed rice and pappadums.
TIP You will need 1 large bunch of spinach for this recipe.

4 WAYS WITH COUSCOUS & POLENTA

PINE NUT AND DRIED FIG COUSCOUS

PREP + COOK TIME 15 MINUTES **SERVES** 4

Bring 1 cup chicken stock to the boil in a medium saucepan. Remove from heat, add 1 cup couscous, cover; stand 5 minutes or until liquid is absorbed, fluffing with a fork occasionally. Stir ⅔ cup coarsely chopped dried figs, ½ cup toasted pine nuts, 2 teaspoons finely grated lemon rind, ¼ cup lemon juice and ¼ cup finely chopped fresh flat-leaf parsley into couscous; season to taste.

TIP Add your favourite dried fruit or nuts to the couscous. Serve warm or cold.

LEMON PISTACHIO COUSCOUS

PREP + COOK TIME 15 MINUTES **SERVES** 4

Combine 1 cup couscous, ¾ cup boiling water, 2 teaspoons finely grated lemon rind and ¼ cup lemon juice in a medium heatproof bowl. Cover; stand 5 minutes or until liquid is absorbed, fluffing with a fork occasionally. Meanwhile, dry-fry ½ cup pistachios in a heated small frying pan until fragrant; remove nuts from pan, chop coarsely. Heat 2 teaspoons olive oil in same pan, add 1 crushed garlic clove and 1 finely chopped small red onion; cook, stirring, until onion softens. Fluff couscous then stir nuts, onion mixture and ½ cup shredded fresh mint through couscous.

CHEESY PESTO POLENTA

PREP + COOK TIME 35 MINUTES **SERVES** 4

Blend or process 2 tablespoons each finely grated parmesan, pine nuts and olive oil, 1 crushed garlic clove and 1 cup firmly packed basil leaves until mixture forms a paste. Combine 2⅓ cups water and 2⅓ cups milk in a large saucepan; bring to the boil. Gradually sprinkle 1 cup polenta over milk mixture; cook, stirring, until polenta thickens slightly. Reduce heat; simmer, uncovered, for 20 minutes or until polenta is thickened, stirring constantly. Stir in ½ cup finely grated parmesan, 30g butter (1 ounce) and pesto. Season to taste.

TIP If you don't want to make your own pesto, use 95g (3 ounces) of the store-bought variety.

SOFT POLENTA

PREP + COOK TIME 20 MINUTES **SERVES** 6

Combine 3 cups milk and 2 cups chicken stock in a large saucepan; bring to the boil. Gradually add 2 cups polenta to liquid, stirring constantly. Reduce heat; simmer, stirring, for 10 minutes or until polenta thickens. Add 1 cup milk and ¼ cup finely grated parmesan, stir until cheese melts.

SPICED CARROT AND KUMARA SOUP

PREP + COOK TIME 9 HOURS SERVES 4

2 medium brown onions (300g), chopped coarsely

5 medium carrots (600g), chopped coarsely

3 small kumara (orange sweet potato) (750g), chopped coarsely

1 tablespoon ground coriander

2 teaspoons cumin seeds

½ teaspoon dried chilli flakes

1 litre (4 cups) salt-reduced chicken stock

2 cups (500ml) water

¾ cup (200g) Greek-style yoghurt

½ cup firmly packed fresh coriander (cilantro) sprigs

1 Place onion, carrot, kumara, ground coriander, cumin, chilli, stock and the water in a 4.5-litre (18-cup) slow cooker. Cook, covered, on low, about 8 hours.
2 Cool soup 10 minutes. Blend or process soup, in batches, until smooth. Return soup to cooker. Cook, covered, on high, for 20 minutes or until hot. Season to taste.
3 To serve, dollop soup with yoghurt and sprinkle with fresh coriander.

SUITABLE TO FREEZE At the end of step 2.
SERVING SUGGESTION Warm naan bread.
TIPS If the soup is too thick add a little more stock or water. Swap chicken stock for vegetable for a vegetarian option.

VEGETABLE HARIRA

PREP + COOK TIME 8 HOURS 45 MINUTES
SERVES 8

2 teaspoons each ground cumin, ground coriander
and sweet smoked paprika

1 teaspoon each ground ginger, ground cinnamon
and dried chilli flakes

¼ teaspoon ground nutmeg

1 large brown onion (200g), chopped finely

2 medium carrots (240g), chopped finely

4 stalks celery (600g), trimmed, chopped finely

5 medium tomatoes (750g), chopped finely

6 cloves garlic, crushed

2 tablespoons tomato paste

1.5 litres (6 cups) vegetable stock

1 litre (4 cups) water

1 cup (200g) French-style green lentils

400g (12½ ounces) canned chickpeas (garbanzo beans),
rinsed, drained

⅓ cup each finely chopped fresh flat-leaf parsley
and coriander (cilantro)

1 Dry-fry spices in a small frying pan over medium
heat for 1 minute or until fragrant.
2 Combine onion, carrot, celery, tomato, garlic, spices,
paste, stock, the water and lentils in a 4.5-litre (18-cup)
slow cooker. Cook, covered, on low, about 8 hours.
Season to taste.
3 Add chickpeas to cooker and stir until heated through.
4 Stir in parsley and coriander to serve.

SUITABLE TO FREEZE At the end of step 3.
SERVING SUGGESTION Lemon wedges and warm flat bread.

PARMESAN, SPINACH AND BEAN RAGU

PREP + COOK TIME 8 HOURS 45 MINUTES **SERVES** 6

375g (12 ounces) dried four-bean mix

50g (1½ ounces) butter, chopped coarsely

1 tablespoon olive oil

1 large brown onion (200g), chopped finely

1 medium carrot (120g), chopped finely

2 stalks celery (300g), trimmed, chopped finely

3 cloves garlic, crushed

½ cup (125ml) dry white wine

2 tablespoons tomato paste

400g (12½ ounces) canned crushed tomatoes

2 cups (500ml) vegetable stock

2 teaspoons sea salt flakes

2 teaspoons caster (superfine) sugar

4 sprigs fresh thyme

50g (1½ ounces) baby spinach leaves

1 cup (80g) finely grated parmesan

1 Place bean mix in a medium saucepan; cover with 5cm (2 inches) cold water. Bring to the boil over medium-low heat. Boil about 5 minutes; drain. Transfer beans to a 4.5-litre (18-cup) slow cooker.

2 Heat butter and oil in a large frying pan over medium heat; cook onion, carrot, celery and garlic, stirring, for 5 minutes or until softened. Add wine; bring to the boil. Boil until wine has almost evaporated. Add paste, tomatoes, stock, salt, sugar and thyme. Transfer to cooker. Cook, covered, on low, about 8 hours. Season to taste.

3 Discard thyme. Stir in spinach until wilted. Sprinkle ragù with parmesan to serve.

SUITABLE TO FREEZE At the end of step 2.
SERVING SUGGESTION Fresh crusty bread.
TIP We used a chardonnay-style wine in this recipe.

4 WAYS WITH RICE

PILAF

PREP + COOK TIME 30 MINUTES **SERVES** 4

Melt 20g (¾ ounce) butter in a medium saucepan; cook 1 crushed garlic clove, stirring, until fragrant. Add 1 cup basmati rice; cook, stirring, about 1 minute. Add 1 cup chicken stock and 1 cup water; bring to the boil. Reduce heat; simmer, covered, for 20 minutes or until rice is just tender. Remove from heat; fluff rice with a fork. Stir in ¼ cup coarsely chopped fresh flat-leaf parsley and ¼ cup toasted flaked almonds.

YELLOW COCONUT RICE

PREP + COOK TIME 30 MINUTES (+ STANDING) **SERVES** 4

Stand 1¾ cups white long grain rice in a large bowl of cold water for 30 minutes. Rinse rice under cold water until water runs clear; drain. Place 1¼ cups water, 1⅔ cups coconut cream, 1 teaspoon each white sugar and salt, ½ teaspoon ground turmeric, a pinch saffron threads and rice in a large heavy-based saucepan; cover, bring to the boil, stirring occasionally. Reduce heat; simmer, covered, without stirring, for 15 minutes or until rice is tender. Remove from heat; stand, covered, 5 minutes. Season to taste.

STEAMED GINGER RICE

PREP + COOK TIME 20 MINUTES **SERVES** 4

Heat 1 tablespoon olive oil in a medium saucepan; cook 6 thinly sliced green onions (scallions), stirring, until softened. Add 2½ teaspoons finely grated fresh ginger and 1½ cups basmati rice; stir to coat in oil. Add 2 cups chicken stock; bring to the boil. Reduce heat; simmer, covered, over low heat, about 10 minutes. Remove from heat; stand, covered, 5 minutes, then fluff with a fork; stir in 2 tablespoons each finely chopped fresh coriander (cilantro) and mint, season to taste.

RICE AND PEAS

PREP + COOK TIME 30 MINUTES **SERVES** 6

Combine 1½ cups water, 1½ cups chicken stock and ¼ cup olive oil in a medium saucepan; bring to the boil. Stir in 2 cups white medium-grain rice; cook, uncovered, without stirring, for 10 minutes or until liquid has almost evaporated. Reduce heat; simmer, covered, about 5 minutes. Meanwhile, thinly slice 4 green onions (scallions). Gently stir in onion and 1 cup frozen peas; simmer, covered, for 5 minutes or until rice and peas are tender. Season to taste.

VEGETABLE STEW

PREP + COOK TIME 9 HOURS SERVES 4

1 medium red onion (170g),
cut into wedges

2 medium zucchini (240g),
sliced thickly

4 yellow patty pan squash (120g),
cut into wedges

1 medium kumara (orange sweet
potato) (400g), chopped coarsely

2 medium carrots (240g),
chopped coarsely

1 trimmed corn cob (250g),
cut into 6 rounds

1 medium red capsicum (bell
pepper) (350g), chopped coarsely

2 flat mushrooms (160g),
cut into wedges

3 cloves garlic, crushed

30g (1-ounce) sachet taco seasoning

2 teaspoons paprika

800g (1½ pounds) canned
crushed tomatoes

1 cup (250ml) vegetable stock

2 tablespoons fresh flat-leaf
parsley leaves

POLENTA DUMPLINGS
1 cup (150g) self-raising flour

2 tablespoons polenta (cornmeal)

60g (2 ounces) cold butter, chopped

1 egg, beaten lightly

¼ cup (20g) finely grated parmesan

2 tablespoons milk, approximately

1   Place onion, zucchini, squash, kumara, carrot, corn, capsicum, mushrooms, garlic, seasoning, paprika, tomatoes and stock in a 4.5-litre (18-cup) slow cooker. Cook, covered, on low, about 8 hours.
2   Make polenta dumpling mixture just before required.
3   Drop level tablespoons of dumpling mixture, about 2cm (¾ inch) apart, on top of stew. Cook, covered, on low, for 30 minutes or until dumplings are firm to touch and cooked through. Serve stew with dumplings and sprinkle with parsley.

POLENTA DUMPLINGS Place flour and polenta in a medium bowl; rub in butter. Stir in egg, parmesan and enough milk to make a soft, sticky dough.

NOT SUITABLE TO FREEZE.
TIP Add rinsed, drained canned kidney beans or trimmed green beans for the last 10 minutes of cooking time.

MOROCCAN CHICKPEA STEW

PREP + COOK TIME 9 HOURS SERVES 4

3 x 400g (12½ ounces) canned chickpeas (garbanzo beans), rinsed, drained

1 large red onion (300g), sliced thinly

3 cloves garlic, crushed

1 fresh long red chilli, chopped finely

1 large carrot (180g), halved, sliced thickly

½ medium cauliflower (750g), cut into large florets

2 tablespoons moroccan seasoning

pinch saffron threads

1 tablespoon honey

400g (12½ ounces) canned diced tomatoes

3 cups (750ml) vegetable or chicken stock

250g (8 ounces) cavolo nero (tuscan cabbage), trimmed, shredded

250g (8 ounces) yellow patty pan squash, halved

1 tablespoon Greek-style yoghurt

2 tablespoons finely sliced preserved lemon rind

⅓ cup loosely packed fresh flat-leaf parsley leaves

1   Combine chickpeas, onion, garlic, chilli, carrot, cauliflower, seasoning, saffron, honey, tomatoes and stock in a 5-litre (20-cup) slow cooker. Cook, covered, on low, about 8 hours.
2   Add cavolo nero and squash to cooker; cook, covered, on high, for 20 minutes or until squash is tender. Season to taste.
3   Serve stew topped with yoghurt and sprinkled with preserved lemon rind and parsley.

SUITABLE TO FREEZE At the end of step 1.
SERVING SUGGESTION Steamed couscous.

4 WAYS WITH MASH

SPINACH MASH

PREP + COOK TIME 30 MINUTES **SERVES** 4

Place 1kg (2 pounds) coarsely chopped peeled potatoes in a medium saucepan with enough cold water to barely cover potato. Boil, uncovered, over medium heat for 15 minutes or until potato is tender; drain. Meanwhile, boil, steam or microwave 200g (6½ ounces) baby spinach leaves until wilted; drain. Squeeze out excess liquid. Blend or process spinach with 40g (1½ ounces) butter until almost smooth. Mash potato; stir in ¼ teaspoon nutmeg, ½ cup hot pouring cream and spinach mixture. Season to taste.

TIP Any all-round or mashing potato is fine to use here. Desiree, pontiac or sebago are good choices.

POTATO PUREE

PREP + COOK TIME 30 MINUTES **SERVES** 4

Place 1kg (2 pounds) coarsely chopped peeled potatoes in a medium saucepan with enough cold water to barely cover the potato. Boil, uncovered, over medium heat, for 15 minutes or until potato is tender; drain. Using the back of a wooden spoon, push potato through a fine sieve into a large bowl. Stir 40g (1½ ounces) butter and ¾ cup hot milk into potato, folding gently until mash is smooth and fluffy.

TIP We used lasoda potatoes, but use any general purpose or mashing variety – desiree, sebago, coliban and king edward are all fine to use.

CELERIAC MASH

PREP + COOK TIME 30 MINUTES **SERVES** 6

Place 800g (1½ pounds) coarsely chopped peeled potatoes in a medium saucepan with enough cold water to barely cover potato. Boil, uncovered, over medium heat for 15 minutes or until potato is tender. Drain. Meanwhile, boil, steam or microwave 1kg (2 pounds) coarsely chopped peeled celeriac (celery root) until tender; drain. Mash potato and celeriac together; stir in 60g (2 ounces) butter and ½ cup hot pouring cream. Drizzle with 2 teaspoons olive oil and sprinkle with cracked black pepper to taste.

KUMARA MASH

PREP + COOK TIME 30 MINUTES **SERVES** 4

Boil, steam or microwave 500g (1 pound) coarsely chopped peeled kumara (orange sweet potato) and 500g (1 pound) coarsely chopped peeled potatoes together until tender; drain. Mash potato and kumara. Combine ¼ cup chicken stock and 40g (1½ ounces) butter in a small saucepan over medium high heat until butter is melted. Stir into kumara mixture until combined. Season to taste.

SILVER BEET DHAL

PREP + COOK TIME 10 HOURS 20 MINUTES **SERVES** 6

500g (1 pound) yellow split peas

45g (1½ ounces) ghee

2 medium brown onions (300g), chopped finely

3 cloves garlic, crushed

4cm (1½-inch) piece fresh ginger (20g), grated

1 fresh long green chilli, chopped finely

2 tablespoons black mustard seeds

1 teaspoon cumin seeds

1 tablespoon ground coriander

2 teaspoons ground turmeric

1 teaspoon garam masala

800g (1½ pounds) canned diced tomatoes

3 cups (750ml) vegetable stock

1½ cups (375ml) water

1 teaspoon caster (superfine) sugar

4 medium silver beet (swiss chard) leaves (320g), stems removed, chopped coarsely

1   Rinse split peas under cold water until water runs clear; drain.
2   Heat ghee in a large frying pan; cook onion, garlic, ginger and chilli, stirring, until onion softens. Add seeds and spices; cook, stirring, until fragrant. Place onion mixture into a 4.5-litre (18-cup) slow cooker; stir in tomatoes, stock, the water, sugar and split peas. Cook, covered, on low, about 10 hours.
3   Stir in silver beet; season to taste.

SUITABLE TO FREEZE At the end of step 2.
SERVING SUGGESTION Top with fried or caramelised onions.

SMOKY CHICKPEA AND TOMATO SOUP

PREP + COOK TIME 8 HOURS 30 MINUTES **SERVES** 6

1.5kg (3 pounds) tomatoes, quartered

1 large brown onion (200g), chopped coarsely

3 cloves garlic, chopped coarsely

1 stalk celery (150g), trimmed, sliced thickly

3 x 400g (12½ ounces) canned chickpeas (garbanzo beans), rinsed, drained

1¾ cups (430ml) chicken stock

2 teaspoons smoked paprika

1 tablespoon caster (superfine) sugar

⅓ cup (80g) sour cream

1   Place tomato, onion, garlic, celery, chickpeas, stock, paprika and sugar in a 4.5-litre (18-cup) slow cooker. Cook, covered, on low, about 8 hours.
2   Using a slotted spoon, transfer 2 cups of the chickpeas to a medium bowl; reserve. Stand remaining soup 10 minutes, then process soup until smooth. Stir in reserved chickpeas. Season to taste.
3   Serve soup topped with sour cream.

SUITABLE TO FREEZE At the end of step 2.
SERVING SUGGESTION Char-grilled bread.
TIP Choose the ripest tomatoes you can find. If you dislike tomato skins, you can either peel the tomatoes before adding to the cooker or strain the pureed soup before returning the chickpeas.

BASIC STOCKS

VEGETABLE

PREP + COOK TIME 1 HOUR 45 MINUTES
MAKES 3.5 LITRES (14 CUPS)

2 large carrots (360g), chopped coarsely

2 large parsnips (700g), chopped coarsely

4 medium onions (600g), chopped coarsely

10 celery stalks (1.5kg), trimmed, chopped coarsely

4 bay leaves

2 teaspoons black peppercorns

6 litres (24 cups) water

1 Combine ingredients in a large saucepan or stockpot; bring to the boil. Reduce heat; simmer, uncovered, about 1½ hours, skimming surface occasionally. Strain stock through a fine sieve into a large heatproof bowl; discard solids. If not using immediately, cool slightly, then refrigerate to cool completely.

BEEF

PREP + COOK TIME 5 HOURS 15 MINUTES
MAKES 3.5 LITRES (14 CUPS)

2kg (4 pounds) meaty beef bones

2 medium brown onions (300g), chopped coarsely

5.5 litres water (22 cups)

2 celery stalks (300g), trimmed, chopped coarsely

2 medium carrots (240g), chopped coarsely

3 bay leaves

2 teaspoons black peppercorns

3 litres water (12 cups), extra

1 Preheat oven to 200°C/400°F.
2 Roast bones for 1 hour or until browned.
3 Transfer bones to a large saucepan or stockpot. Add onion, the water, vegetables, bay leaves and peppercorns; bring to the boil. Reduce heat; simmer, uncovered, about 3 hours, skimming surface occasionally. Add extra water; simmer, uncovered, about 1 hour. Strain stock through a fine sieve into a large heatproof bowl; discard solids. If not using immediately, cool slightly, then refrigerate stock to cool completely. Skim and discard surface fat before using.

CHICKEN

PREP + COOK TIME 2 HOURS 15 MINUTES
MAKES 3.5 LITRES (14 CUPS)

2kg (4 pounds) chicken bones

2 medium onions (300g), chopped coarsely

2 celery stalks (300g), trimmed, chopped coarsely

2 medium carrots (240g), chopped coarsely

3 bay leaves

2 teaspoons black peppercorns

5 litres (20 cups) water

1 Combine ingredients in a large saucepan or stockpot; bring to the boil. Reduce heat; simmer, uncovered, about 2 hours, skimming surface occasionally. Strain stock through a fine sieve into a large heatproof bowl; discard solids. If not using immediately, cool slightly, then refrigerate stock to cool completely. Skim and discard surface fat before using.

TIP STORE HOMEMADE STOCK REFRIGERATED, FOR UP TO 1 WEEK, OR IN THE FREEZER FOR UP TO 1 MONTH. BRING TO THE BOIL BEFORE USING.

GLOSSARY

ALL SPICE also known as pimento or jamaican pepper; available whole or ground. Tastes like a blend of cinnamon, clove and nutmeg — all spices.

BACON SLICES also known as bacon rashes; made from cured, smoked pork.

BEANS

borlotti also called roman beans or pink beans; available both fresh and dried. Interchangeable with pinto beans due to their similarity in appearance - pale pink or beige with dark red streaks.

broad (fava) also called windsor and horse beans; available dried, fresh, canned and frozen. Fresh should be peeled twice (discarding the outer long green pod and the beige-green tough inner shell); frozen beans have had their pods removed but the beige shell still needs removal.

butter also known as lima beans; large, flat, kidney-shaped bean, off-white in colour, with a mild taste. Available canned and dried, and fresh in the pod.

cannellini a small white bean similar in appearance and flavour to other white beans (great northern, navy or haricot), all of which can be substituted for the other. Available dried or canned.

kidney medium-sized red bean, slightly floury in texture, yet sweet in flavour.

sprouts also known as bean shoots; tender new growths of assorted beans and seeds germinated for consumption.

white a generic term we use for canned or dried cannellini, haricot, navy or great northern beans. All these beans are of the same family and can be substituted for the other.

BEEF

brisket a cheaper cut from the belly; available with our without bones as a joint for slow roasting, or for stewing as casseroling as cubes or mince.

blade taken from the shoulder; isn't as tender as other cuts, so needs slow roasting for best results.

cheeks the cheek muscle. A very tough and lean cut of meat, often used for braising or slow cooking to produce a tender result.

chuck from the neck and shoulder; tends to be chewy but flavourful and inexpensive. A good cut for strewing or braising.

corned silverside also known as topside roast; sold vacuum-sealed in brine.

gravy beed also known as beef shin or shank; cut from the lower shin.

osso buco literally meaning 'bone with a hole', osso buco is cut from the shin of the hind leg. It is also known as knuckle.

sausages seasoned and spiced mince (ground) beef mixed with cereal and packed into casings.

shank see gravy beef, above.

short ribs cut from the rub section; usually larger, more tender and meatier than pork spare ribs.

BEETROOT (beets) also known as red beets; a firm, round root vegetable.

BUK CHOY also known as bok choy, pak choi, chinese white cabbage or chinese chard; has a fresh, mild mustard taste. Use both stems and leaves. Baby buk choy, also known as pak kat farang or shanghai bok choy, is smaller and more tender than buk choy.

BUTTER use salted or unsalted (sweet) butter; 125g is equal to one stick of butter (4 ounces).

CAPERS grey-green buds of a warm climate shrub (usually Mediterranean); sold dried and salted or pickled in a vinegar brine. Baby capers, those picked early, are very small, fuller-flavoured and more expensive than the full-size ones. Capers, whether packed in brine or in salt, must be rinsed well before using.

CAPSICUM (bell pepper) also known as just 'pepper'. Comes in many colours: red, green, yellow, orange and purplish-black. Be sure to discard seeds and membranes before use.

CARAWAY a member of the parsley family; is available in seed or ground form. Has a pungent aroma and a distinctly sweet, but tangy flavour.

CARDOMAN purchase in a pod, seed or ground form. Has a pungent aroma.

CHICKEN

drumsticks leg with skin and bone attached.

thigh cutlets thigh with skin and centre bone intact; sometimes found skinned with bone intact.

thigh fillets thigh with skin and bone removed.

CHILLI available in many types and sizes. Use rubber gloves when seeding and chopping fresh chillis as they can burn your skin. Removing membranes and seeds lessens the heat level.

cayenne pepper dried, long, thin-fleshed, extremely hot ground red chilli.

flakes dried, deep-red, dehydrated chilli slices and whole seeds.

long green any unripened chilli.

long red available both fresh and dried; a generic term used for any moderately hot, thin, long chilli.

powder can be used as a substitute for fresh chillis (½ teaspoon ground chilli powder to 1 medium chopped fresh chilli).

CORIANDER the leaves, stems and roots of coriander are used in Thai cooking; wash roots well before using. Is also available ground or as seeds; do not substitute these for fresh coriander as the tastes are completely different.

COUSCOUS a fine, dehydrated, grain-like cereal product made from semolina; it swells to about three or four times its original size when liquid is added. Often used as a side-dish to accompany Middle-Eastern meals. .

CREAM we use fresh cream, also known as pure cream and pouring cream, unless otherwise stated.

CUMIN a spice also known as zeera or comino; has a spicy, nutty flavour, and is available in seed form or dried or ground.

CURRY LEAVES available in fresh or dried and have a mild curry flavour; use like bay leaves.

CURRY PASTES some recipes in this book call for commercially prepared pastes of varying strengths and flavours. Use whichever one you feel best suits your spice-level tolerance.

korma paste a mix of mostly heat-free spices; forms the base of a mild, almost nutty, slow-cooked curry.

powder a blend of ground spices that include chilli, cinnamon, coriander, mace, fennel, cumin, fenugreek, cardamon and tumeric.

red probably the most popular curry paste; a blend of red chilli, garlic, shallot, lemon grass, salt, galangal, shrimp paste, kaffir lime peel, coriander, cumin and paprika. It is milder than the hotter thai green curry paste.

rogan josh a medium-hot blend that is a speciality of Kashmir in northern India. It contains tomatoes, fenugreek, coriander, paprika and cumin.

vindaloo a very hot curry flavoured with tamarind, vinegar and garlic.

EGGPLANT also known as aubergine.

FLOUR

cornflour also known as cornstarch; used as a thickening agent. Available as 100% corn (maize) and wheaten cornflour.

plain all-purpose flour made from wheat.

self-raising plain flour sifted with baking powder in the proportion of 1 cup flour to 2 teaspoons baking powder.

GINGER also known as green or root ginger; the thick root of a tropical plant.

GRAVY POWDER an instant gravy mix made with browned flour. Plain flour can be used instead for thickening. Available from supermarkets in a variety of flavours.

HARISSA a Moroccan paste made from dried chillis, cumin, garlic, oil and caraway seeds. Available from Middle-Eastern food shops and some supermarkets.

KAFFIR LIME LEAVES also known as bai magrood, sold fresh, dried or frozen; looks like two glossy dark green leaves joined end to end, forming a rounded hourglass shape. A strip of fresh lime peel may be substituted for each kaffir lime leaf.

KUMARA Polynesian name of an orange-fleshed sweet potato often confused with yam.

LAMB

forequarter chops cut from the shoulder end.

shanks, french-trimmed also known as drumsticks or frenched shanks; the gristle and narrow end of the bone is discarded then the remaining meat is trimmed.

shoulder cut from the shoulder. Is very hard to carve with the bone in; to make carving easier, butchers will bone it and sell it as a boneless rolled shoulder.

LEEK a member of the onion family; looks like a giant green onion but is more mild in flavour

baby, or pencil leeks; essentially younger, slender leeks available early in the season.

LENTILS (red, brown, yellow) dried pulses identified by and named after thier colour.

MARSALA a sweet, fortified wine to which additional alcohol has been added; most commonly in the form of brandy. It is available in a range of styles, from sweet to dry.

MINCE also known as ground meat.

MOROCCAN SEASONING available from most Middle-Eastern food stores, spice

shops and major supermarkets. Tumeric, cinnamon and cumin add authentic Morrocan flavouring to dishes.

MUSHROOMS

button small, mild, cultivated white mushrooms.

enoki has clumps of long, spaghetti-like stems with tiny, snowy white caps.

oyster also known as abalone; grey-white mushrooms shaped like a fan. Prized for thier smooth texture and subtle, oyster-like flavour.

portobello these are mature swiss browns. Large dark brown mushrooms with full-bodied flavour, ideal for filling or barbecueing.

shiitake when fresh are also known as chinese black, forest or golden oak mushrooms. Are large and mealy and, although cultivated, have the earthiness and taste of wild mushrooms.

swiss brown also known as cremini or roman mushrooms, light brown mushrooms having a full-bodied flavour. Substitute button or cup mushrooms for swiss browns.

OILS

olive made from ripened olives. Extra virgin and virgin are the best, while extra light or light refers to taste, not fat levels.

peanut pressed from ground peanuts; most commonly used oil in Asian cooking because of its high smoke point (capacity to handle high heat without burning).

sesame roasted, crushed, white sesame seeds; used as a flavouring rather than a cooking medium.

vegetable sourced from plants.

ONIONS

baby also known as pickling onions and cocktail onions; are baby brown onions, though are larger than shallots.

brown and white are interchangeable, however white onions have a more pungent flesh.

green also known as scallion or, incorrectly, shallot; an immature onion picked before the bulb has formed, having a long, green stalk.

red also known as spanish, red spanish or bermuda onion; a sweet-flavoured, large, purple-red onion.

shallots also called french shallots, golden shallots or eschalots; small, brown-skinned, elongated members of the onion family. Grows in tight clusters similar to garlic.

spring an onion with a small white bulb and long, narrow green-leafed tops.

PAPRIKA ground, dried, sweet red capsicum (bell pepper); there are many types available; including sweet, hot, mild and smoked.

POLENTA also known as cornmeal; a ground, flour-like cereal made of dried corn (maize). Also the name of the dish made from it.

PORK

ham hock the lower portion of the leg; includes the meat, fat and bone. Most have been cured, smoked or both.

neck sometimes called pork scotch; a boneless cut from the foreloin.

pancetta an Italian unsmoked bacon; pork belly cured in salt and spices then rolled into a sausage shape and dried for several weeks. Used, sliced or chopped, as an ingredient rather than eaten on its own.

proscuitto cured, unsmoked, pressed ham.

sausage, italian pork available as both sweet, which is flavoured with garlic and fennel seed, and hot, which has chilli.

shoulder joint sold with bone in or out.

spare ribs (american-style spareribs); well-trimmed mid-loin ribs.

PRESERVED LEMON RIND a North African specialty; lemons are quartered and preserved in salt and lemon juice or water. To use, remove and discard pulp, squeeze juice from rind, then rinse rind well and slice thinly. Sold in delicatessens and supermarkets.

RAS EL HANOUT a classic spice blend used in Moroccan cooking. The name means 'top of the shop' and is the very best spice blend a spice merchant has to offer. Most versions contain over a dozen spices, including cardomom, mace, nutmeg, cinnamon and ground chilli.

RICE

basmati a white, fragrant long-grained rice. Traditionally from India or Pakistan. Wash several times before cooking.

medium-grain previosly sold as calrose rice; an extremely versatile rice that can be substituted for short - or long-grain rices if necessary.

SAUCES

char sui a Chinese barbecue sauce made from sugar, water, salt, fermented soya bean paste, honey, soy sauce, malt syrup and spices. Found at most supermarkets.

fish also called nam pla or nuoc nam; made from pulverised salted fermented fish, most often anchovies. Has a very pungent smell and strong taste, so use according to your taste level.

light soy, a fairly thin, pale but salty tasting sauce: used in dishes where the natural colour of the ingredients is to be maintained. Not to be confused with salt-reduced or low-sodium soy sauces.

oyster Asian in origin, this rich, brown sauce is made from oysters and thier brine, cooked with salt and soy sauce, and thickened with starches.

soy also known as sieu, is made from fermented soya beans. Several variations are available in most supermarkets and Asian food stores. We use a mild Japanese variety in our recipes.

tamari a dark soy sauce made from soya beans, but without the wheat used in most soy sauces.

tomato pasta made from a blend of tomatoes, herbs and spices.

worchestershire a dark-coloured condiment made from garlic, soy sauce, tamarind, onions, molasses, lime, anchovies, vinegar and seasonings

SILVERBEET also known as swiss chard and mistakenly called spinach; a member of the beet family grown for its tasty green leaves and celery-like stems. Best cooked rather than eaten raw. Also known as blettes.

SOUR CREAM a thick commercially-cultured soured cream. Minimum fat content 35%.

SPLIT PEAS a variety of yellow or green peas grown for drying. When dried, the peas usually split along a natural seam. Whole and split dried peas are available packaged in supermarkets and in health-food stores.

STAR ANAISE dried, star-shaped pod having an astringent aniseed flavour; used to flavour stocks and marinades. Available whole and ground, it is an essential ingredient in five-spice powder.

TOMATOES

egg also called plum or roma; a smallish, oval-shaped tomato.

paste triple-concentrated tomato puree.

puree canned pureed tomatoes. Not to be confused with tomato paste. Substitute with fresh peeled and pureed tomatoes.

TORTILLAS thin, round unleavened bread originating in Mexico. Two types are available, one made from wheat flour, the other made from corn.

TUMERIC, GROUND a member of the ginger family, its root is dried and ground, resulting in the rich yellow powder that gives many Indian dishes their characteristic yellow colour. It is intensely pungent in taste, but not hot.

YOGHURT we use plain yoghurt unless otherwise indicated in the recipe.

ZUCCHINI also known as courgette; small green, yellow or white vegetable belonging to the squash family.

INDEX

B

baked beans
  boston baked beans 75
beef
  beef and vegetable soup 33
  beef casserole with cheesy herb
    dumplings 11
  beef, date and spinach tagine 12
  beef pot roast 26
  beef rib bourguignon 24
  beef and thyme beef cheeks 25
  best cuts to use 5
  borscht 39
  bourbon-glazed beef ribs 8
  chilli con carne 30
  chinese braised beef cheeks 19
  coconut curried beef 29
  coriander beef curry 35
  massaman beef curry 17
  mexican beef chilli mole 20
  old-fashioned curried sausages 36
  osso buco with mixed mushrooms 15
  oxtail stew with red wine and port 23
  pulled beef with barbecue sauce 16
  vietnamese beef brisket 32
browning instructions 5

C

chicken
  best cuts to use 5
cooking instructions 5

couscous
  lemon pistachio couscous 94
  pine nut and dried fig couscous 94
curry
  coconut curried beef 29
  coriander beef curry 35
  lamb and baby eggplant curry with cashew
    and coconut 51
  lamb, kumara and almond curry 48
  lamb shank and spinach korma curry 62
  massaman beef curry 17
  old-fashioned curried sausages 36
  peppered pork curry 74
  pork vindaloo 86
  red pork and lychee curry 85
  split pea and capsicum curry 92

D

dumplings
  cheesy herb dumplings 11
  polenta dumplings 102

G

gremolata 68

L

lamb
  best cuts to use 5
  cassoulet 55
  fetta, lemon and herb rolled lamb 42
  greek-style dill and lemon lamb
    shoulder 52

lamb and baby eggplant curry with
  cashews 51
lamb and rosemary stew 49
lamb birria 56
lamb biryani-style 45
lamb, kumara and almond curry 48
lamb shank and spinach korma curry 62
lamb shank, fennel and vegetable soup 46
lancashire hot pot 65
morrocan lamb with honey 58
sicilian meatballs in spicy tomato sauce 61
spicy mexican lamb stew 56
tomato and balsamic lamb stew 59

M

mash
  celeriac mash 107
  kumara mash 107
  potato puree 106
  spinach mash 106
meatballs
  sicilian meatballs in spicy tomato sauce 61

P

paste
  korma paste 62
polenta
  cheesy pesto polenta 95
  polenta dumplings 102
  soft polenta 95

pork
    best cuts to use 5
    best-ever bolognese sauce 76
    boston baked beans 75
    ham and green lentil soup with
        gremolata 68
    honey and balsamic braised pork 80
    italian pork and capsicum ragu 83
    mexican pull-apart pork 82
    peppered pork curry 74
    pork and chilli stew 89
    pork vindaloo 86
    red pork and lychee curry 85
    ribollita 72
    soy pork with mushrooms 79
    sweet and sour italian pork
        with capsicum 71

R

rice
    pilaf 100
    rice and peas 101
    steamed ginger rice 101
    yellow coconut rice 100

S

sauce
    best-ever bolognese sauce 76
slow cooker instructions 5
soup
    beef and vegetable soup 33
    borscht 39

(soup continued)
    ham and green lentil soup with
        gremolata 68
    lamb shank, fennel and vegetable soup 46
    ribollita 72
    smoky chickpea and tomato soup 111
    spiced carrot and kumara soup 96
    vegetable harira 97
stew
    lamb and rosemary stew 49
    moroccan chickpea stew 105
    oxtail stew with red wine and port 23
    pork and chilli stew 89
    spicy mexican lamb stew 56
    tomato and balsamic
        lamb stew 59
    vegetable stew with polenta
        dumplings 102
stock
    beef 112
    chicken 113
    storage tip 113
    vegetable 112

V

veal
    best cuts to use 5
vegetables
    beef stock 112
    boston baked beans 75
    celeriac mash 107
    cheesy pesto polenta 95
    chicken stock 113

(vegetables continued)
    kumara mash 107
    lemon pistachio couscous 94
    moroccan chickpea stew 105
    parmesan, spinach and bean ragu 99
    pilaf 100
    pine nut and dried fig couscous 94
    potato puree 106
    rice and peas 101
    silver beet dhal 108
    smoky chickpea and tomato soup 111
    soft polenta 95
    spiced carrot and kumara soup 96
    spinach mash 106
    split pea and capsicum curry 92
    steamed ginger rice 101
    vegetable harira 97
    vegetable stew 102
    vegetable stock 112
    yellow coconut rice 100

This book is published in 2016 by Octopus Publishing Group Limited based on materials licensed to it by Bauer Media Books, Australia
Bauer Media Books is a division of Bauer Media Pty Limited. 54 Park St, Sydney; GPO Box 4088, Sydney, NSW 2001, Australia
phone (+61) 2 9282 8618; fax (+61) 2 9126 3702 www.awwcookbooks.com.au

BAUER MEDIA BOOKS

Publisher Jo Runciman

Editorial & food director Pamela Clark

Director of sales, marketing & rights Brian Cearnes

Creative director Hannah Blackmore

Designer Luke Atkinson

Editor Erin Mayo

Food editor Rebecca Meli

Operations manager David Scotto

Published and distributed in the United Kingdom by

Octopus Publishing Group Ltd

Carmelite House

50 Victoria Embankment

London, EC4Y 0DZ

United Kingdom

info@octopus-publishing.co.uk;

www.octopusbooks.co.uk

Printed by Leo Paper Products Ltd, China.

International foreign language rights

Brian Cearnes, Bauer Media Books bcearnes@bauer-media.com.au

A catalogue record for this book is available from the British Library.

ISBN: 9781742457260 (paperback)

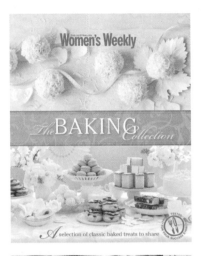
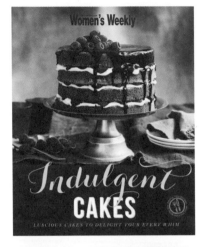

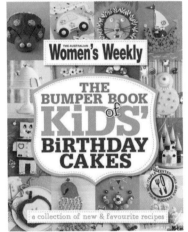